HOW *NOT* TO CATCH A STEER

The steer charged forward at David, who jumped to his left, sideways, through the hedge at James and me. The second steer charged straight for the open gate, where we happened to be standing. I had a vivid impression of a large, heavy red beast very close to me and I seemed to be falling down. This impression was accompanied by a strong barnyard odor. James, I noted, had contrived to fall into the standing corn for a softer landing. That's what a college education will do for you. Just as I raised my head, David dashed through the hedge and fell on top of me, dusty, bruised and dirty but otherwise intact . . .

GORILLA
IN THE
GARAGE
...and other stories

DON HEPWORTH

SMP

ST. MARTIN'S PAPERBACKS

Published by arrangement with Jack McLelland & Associates

GORILLA IN THE GARAGE . . . AND OTHER STORIES

ISBN: 0-312-92117-9

Printed in the United States of America

Boston Mills edition published 1987
St. Martin's Paperbacks edition/April 1990

10 9 8 7 6 5 4 3 2 1

We wish to acknowledge the financial assistance and encouragement of the Canada Council, the Ontario Arts Council and the Office of the Secretary of State.

CONTENTS

Flory's Farewell to Algoma 1
The Naughty Lady of Shady Lane 11
The Tiger Man 18
Lost Property and the Spider Bandit: 28
A Tale in Three Parts
Go Forth and Multiply 42
The Hermit of Oak Tree Hill 49
The King City Roundup 56
Hippie Beef 62
The Great Killaloe Pig Fight 66
A Horse of a Different Colour 73
The North York Lion 93
The Epic of Muffin Inlet 104
A Singed Nightingale 114
A Jaguar for Christmas 127
The Seaway Zoo 137
The Pet Motel 154
Trouble at the Back End 163
Not in the Public Interest 172
The Lakeland Dog Massacre 193
Circus Circus 200
Little Dog Lost 210
The Gorilla in the Garage 216

FLORY'S
FAREWELL
TO ALGOMA

THE SNAKE HAS BEEN AN OBJECT OF FASCINATION AND worship since prehistoric times, and it seems the greater the snake, the more fascinated man is with it. When the Australian Aborigines hold fertility festivals, they paint themselves to resemble snakes so that the number of edible snakes in the area will increase. Since the snakes provide food, the tribe will thereby also thrive. The Toltec peoples of Mexico worshipped Quetzalcoatl, the feathered serpent god of civilization. The snake is a phallic symbol for the Hindus of India, and poisonous snakes were once employed as executioners by some rajahs of old. There were Norman lords in medieval England who weren't above using adders as part-time tax collectors, as these instructions remind us: "Imprission ye malefactor in some convenient dungeon. Throw in several adders. Vassals with but a poor memory as to the whereabouts of their coin will instantly be cured of ye (amnesia)."

One morning in August the OPP phoned to ask me what I knew about snakes. This particular OPP detachment, it seemed, had a snake problem. Not just any old snake, but a monstrous and exotic one, the former mascot of a motorcycle gang. According to what the OPP told me, the gang had purchased the reptile on a drug-buying expedition to the southern United States. Drugs in bulk had been secreted in a box that also contained the snake. What customs officer would consider disturbing a large snake? That, no doubt, was what the motorcycle gang had asked themselves. They had given themselves the wrong answer.

The gang had been sentenced to imprisonment for drug smuggling. The only one of them that remained at liberty was the large snake, described by the officer as "probably an anaconda," presently being accommodated in a building in Northern Ontario. His Honour, the sentencing judge, had directed the officer in the case to "get the Humane Society to take it away."

I noted that the judge had not specified who was to take it, where it was to be taken, or, most importantly, how. I acknowledged the OPP request and said vaguely, "Somebody will be up to attend to it."

Someone had to make a trip to Northern Ontario and bring back a large and dangerous snake. As we were at the peak of summer vacation time, with everyone busy, I had the distinct and depressing feeling the someone was me. I discussed the situation with the Society's director.

"Who is underwriting the cost?" he asked, always his first question.

"It was a court order," I said. "The Attorney General will have to foot the bill."

"Good thinking," the director congratulated me.

My flight arrived and I rented a car. When I presented myself at the Glen Evans OPP detachment's office, the officers were delighted to see me. An officer was detailed to assist me, and together we drove out to a semi-derelict farm some twenty miles out of town.

It was a warm, still day. "The warmer the weather, the livelier the snake," I reflected as we drove along. (They are technically homotherms. Unlike so-called warm-blooded animals, they have no thermostats to keep their body temperatures stable. Consequently, their body temperatures are roughly the same as that of their environment. Their metabolism and level of activity vary accordingly.)

The car stopped in the farmyard. "Your snake is in here," said the officer. He'd already bequeathed it to me, it seemed, whether or not I wanted it or could figure out how to remove it. We walked into a corrugated steel garage after the officer had unlocked the chained doors. There, in a large pit six feet deep, was the snake, barely perceptible in the dimness of the garage.

We pushed the doors wide open and switched on the lights. I wanted to observe this beast under the best possible conditions. The pit was roughly rectangular, following the inside dimensions of half the drive shed, making it more than twenty-five feet long by ten feet wide. The walls of the pit were strengthened with industrial plastic sheeting, reinforced with snow-fencing pegged into the earth. The floor was the bare, sandy soil of the Algoma region.

In the far corner, coiled but aware of us, lay the huge snake, its head lifted slightly, forked tongue flicking in and out, sampling the smell of us. By flicking the sample to the Jacobsen's organs in the roof of its mouth, the animal had smelled us. The scent-sensitive organs had by now identified us as warm mammals who just might be a welcome meal.

Hunting around the shed, I found a pole and a stepladder long enough to reach the pit floor. I used the pole first, prodding the snake experimentally. As it uncoiled and moved out of range, I counted the sections of snow-fencing it passed. Four and a half four-foot sections. The snake was eighteen feet long. I realized I had a python on my hands. The tiny limb vestiges were visible, but I was unsure whether I had an Indian or African species to deal with. Either way it was still a python. The mid-section was as thick as my thigh, and I used to play rugby. I guessed its weight at two hundred pounds.

The OPP had supplied me with a large bag made of stout canvas. The question was how to get the python into it.

"What are you going to do?" asked the officer.

"Feed it," I told him. "Feed it a good meal. It will quietly swallow whole whatever I give it. Its stomach will distend while it peacefully enjoys the digestive process, and at that point I'll ease it into the canvas bag and ship it down to Toronto."

The officer beamed happily. "Simple, why didn't we think of that? You guys must know everything about animals."

I smiled and nodded. Silently I was thinking that so far I'd managed to avoid this particular species.

We drove to a nearby chicken farm, where I paid the farmer fifty cents each for six dead chickens. They had all expired that morning and were soft and still warm. Returning to the snake, I dropped the half-dozen dead birds in a pile in the centre of the pit. I reasoned it would be easier to ease the beast into my sack if I could work round it from any direction and at the greatest possible distance.

The snake uncoiled and undulated its way to the chickens. The tongue flicked repeatedly. It recoiled, still flicking its tongue, as if it were thinking over the repast I had provided. After some twenty minutes it had not yet begun to feed.

"Let's go have lunch," suggested the officer. I looked at my watch. It was one-thirty already. We drove off to a modest teetotal eatery, where I had a sandwich and tea, and gave some thought to naming my snake.

An hour later we returned, only to find the dead birds untouched and the snake back in its favourite corner. I asked the officer if he knew what the gang had fed "Florence," as I had decided to name the python. After some conversation on his car radio, he told me the gang had fed her live young pigs. Obviously she was accustomed to a live porcine diet. It would take ten, perhaps fourteen days to accustom her to taking dead feed. I didn't have the time and the Society couldn't stand the expense. I would have to expedite things. We were preparing to leave when I had an idea.

"Leave the doors open," I said.

The officer grew perturbed. "I can't do that," he replied. "What if some kids come by and fall in the pit?"

"No kids have a right to be here."

"True, but suppose they did come and suppose they fell into the pit?"

"Suppose they fell into the river." We were getting nowhere. "Look," I said, "I have to move this bloody reptile. I didn't ask for the job. Did you see me with my hand up volunteering? Now, I want that beast to be cold tomorrow. I mean *cold*. And I'm hoping it will be cool tonight. That's the only way she'll be safe to handle."

The police agreed to leave the door open, but they insisted that someone be stationed there in a car to guard against innocent trespassers.

We drove to the local safety supply company, where I purchased two CO_2 or carbon dioxide fire extinguishers. Carbon dioxide in a solid state is dry ice. It becomes a solid upon combining with oxygen—that is, after it has left the fire extinguisher. I planned to spray the snake with it. By my line of reasoning, the python would cool down, its muscles would stiffen, it would contract, and it would be safe to handle. I hoped.

I also needed a wooden crate in addition to the canvas bag. From experience I know carpenters are too busy to make good strong packing cases on short notice. I went to the local undertaker. He seemed a trifle perplexed that we didn't have anyone to bury—at least not just then. I explained I wanted to rent a "case." This is the name given to the long box in which a coffin (body within) is housed when shipment is required. Basically, a "case" is a very strong, plain packing case. We arranged for one to be delivered to the farm between six and seven o'clock that evening. This was becoming a pricey job.

It was decided I would stay the night at a local hostelry and we would all meet at the farm at five in the morning. First I had a bath, and after that a hearty meal. I was just about to pay my dinner bill and leave for my room when a voice from the past reached through my ears and into my soul. The voice belonged to Rob Roy McGregor, who was staying at the same motel.

I had known McGregor some years ago in England,

when he had been the senior corporal piper in the Scots Guards. He had been waiting to fill a sergeant's shoes, literally, when the sergeant shuffled off one way or another. With the cessation of World War II, promotion had slowed a trifle. Korea had erupted, but the Household Brigade didn't get involved in common brawls like that, so Rob Roy had remained a corporal for eight long years. One day, to his surprise, an officer from the Royal Canadian Air Force had called on the regiment and asked for him. It seemed the RCAF needed a leading piper and Rob Roy was their choice. Since then he had instructed, coached and adjudicated wherever in Canada the great Highland bagpipe was played. He happened to be in this Northern town to render his expertise. When I told him my occupation and reason for being there, he was intrigued. We had a dram of Glenfiddich on it.

Looking at my watch, I noticed it was about time for the box to be delivered from the undertaker. I invited Rob Roy to come along for the ride, and he brought his bagpipes with him.

We arrived at the farm to the tune of "The Barren Rocks of Aden." The solitary constable on guard was incredulous. Here was the snake-catcher accompanied by a kilted bagpiper. If he noticed the aroma of Scottish wine, he was too polite to mention it.

"Ah'll gie him a blo'," Rob Roy rumbled. He struck up with "Black Bear." Just then the coffin box arrived. I signed for it. The driver wasn't inclined to linger. If his expression was a true indicator, he was ready to believe he'd chanced upon a madhouse. Perhaps he had.

The constable and I then sat on the coffin box, keeping time to the pipes with our tapping feet. Rob Roy was marching round and round the pit edge, playing a part of his repertoire. No one can resist a master piper sounding "The Earl of Mansfield," "Lowdens Woods," "The Fairy Dance," or "Corn Rigs," but Flory moved not an inch.

"What's the matter wi' him," Rob Roy wondered. "When we were in India they fellahs would get the snakes

up wi' a wee chanter thingy. This fellah dean't dea nowt."
I explained snakes were deaf and it was the snake charmer's swaying that moved the snakes Rob Roy had seen in India.

"Nooo! That canna be! I'll just gae doon and wake him oop." With a good deal of difficulty we dissuaded Rob Roy from this plan. "Paddy's Leather Britches" assaulted the night air as we drove away.

"Anywha! Wha ye call her Floory?" Rob Roy demanded, finally abandoning his pipes.

"Because she's always on the floor," I replied. "If she were a tree snake we'd call her Treesa."

"Wha tha not call her Crawley? She's creepy enough!"

When we returned to the hotel Rob Roy enjoyed several more drams before he went off to his high school competition. I checked the weather report. Possibility of frost, the weatherman was saying. My word, I thought, the snake might get *too* cold and die.

I telephoned the front desk. "Are the stores in town closed?" "Yes," the clerk told me, "five minutes ago, at nine." Definitely worried, I put the phone down and had a think. The snake needed to be kept warm overnight. Nature never intended her for northern climes. I phoned the hotel manager. "Do you by any chance have an electric blanket I could use?"

"Our rooms are thermostatically controlled, sir," he replied proudly.

"Yes, I know, but I urgently need an electric blanket to keep my snake warm."

"Your snake?" he gasped. I pictured him ashen-faced.

"Oh, it's not here," I assured him. "It's at some distance from the hotel." After negotiation, the manager agreed to lend me an electric blanket and a power cable to connect it to the Hydro plug.

Returning to the snake pit, I dropped the blanket in and spread it out by the corners with the long pole. I connected up the power line to an outlet. After several minutes Flory felt the heat source and slithered over. She coiled herself comfortably. I drove back to the hotel and went to bed.

My early call at four-fifteen the next morning arrived all too early. The hotel had managed to see that I had some coffee brought me. I shaved moodily, put on a warm shirt and pullover, donned my navy blue overalls and went out to the fresh morning air. It was damned fresh.

I remember someone once saying that the prospect of being hanged concentrates a man's mind wonderfully. Although I wasn't to be hanged, there was a good possibility I might be killed. I can assure you that you do appreciate the fresh air and the scents of the morning with that prospect in mind. I'm not over-dramatizing, either. Four years after the events related here, a man performing an act with his eight-foot boa was strangled. He died in front of his audience at a nightclub in the Laurentians.

As I drove once more to the farm, I rehearsed in my mind what I would do. The trip this time was all too short. I arrived to find three reluctant heroes who had been detailed to help me. They smiled nervously as we talked and repeatedly pointed out that they had absolutely no experience in handling snakes. I smiled back. I didn't want to disillusion them by telling them I hadn't either.

Florence was coiled on the hotel's fine electric blanket. She looked comfortable and self-satisfied. In fact she looked smug.

I shook out my canvas snake bag, which was really a double-sized mailbag. Carrying the bag, one fire extinguisher and a large bath towel, I slowly descended the ladder into the pit. The three constables craned their heads over the pit edge to watch me. One man held the spare extinguisher and one held a riot shotgun at the ready. I wound the towel several times around my left arm and taped it securely in place. A constricting snake's method of attack is to bite and then hang on, coiling itself around the neck and chest area of its prey. When the coils are tight and the victim is in danger of suffocating, the reptile unhinges its lower jaw and starts to engulf the prey face and head first. The victim expires as he is being swallowed and digested.

We had unplugged the electric blanket before my descent into the pit. My wrapped arm was crooked ready to receive the bite. I walked slowly up behind the snake's head and pulled the blanket out from under her. I fanned her great length with the foam from the fire extinguisher, and her movements slowed and finally stopped.

I grabbed her firmly with both hands just behind the head. I could just about lift four feet of Flory off the ground. She was very slowly trying to uncoil so that she could coil again—around me. "Come on, you guys!" I panted. "Let's get her into the bag."

The three constables tumbled down the ladder and joined me in the pit. I asked the smallest one to hold onto the tail-end of Flory while the two larger men held the thicker middle sections. We began to coil Florence into the spread-open sack. All the time I kept a firm hold on the heavily muscled neck. Her green eyes were unblinking. They seemed to bore holes in my face. She was "Kaa" of Kipling's *Jungle Book* with a vengeance. Our efforts finally succeeded and I was the only one holding any snake not in the bag. Two of the officers held up the sides of the sack. One man held its sliding cords, awaiting my direction.

"Ready?"

"Ready," he replied.

"On the word, pull!" I continued coiling the snake's head into the centre of the sack. "One, two, three, *pull!*" On the count of three I threw the flat head and neck downwards onto the coiled body and let go. The sack closed over it. Florence was caught and I was alive to tell this tale.

We tied the sack securely, hoisted it up the pit's flat sides and locked it in the coffin box. I gathered up the electric blanket, towel and other items I had brought, loading them into the car. We turned off the lights. The box was hauled by the detachment's four-wheel-drive and trailer to the CNR station, and we all went for breakfast.

Rob Roy joined us as we munched corned-beef hash with a fried egg and gallons of coffee. Nothing improves my appetite like a dodgy job successfully done. It was still a beautiful day.

Checking my watch I saw that it was almost train time. I made my excuses and went to load and dispatch Florence on her trip south. Rob Roy came with me, carrying his pipes as usual.

He played as we loaded Florence into the baggage car. He was still playing when the train slowly gathered speed and moved out of the station. The tune was catchy but unfamiliar. I checked out of the motel, said goodbye to Rob Roy and flew south myself.

Florence arrived late afternoon the next day. By nightfall she was settled in a reptile foundation, warm, moist and being broken to dead feed. I missed Rob Roy, but we'd gone our separate ways once again. In fact he dropped out of my memory until one Sunday evening sometime later.

If I'm home Sundays, I always listen between six and seven in the evening to recorded concerts of brass and military music on the radio. The program is presented by a radio man with a good voice, well-timed delivery and wonderful musical sense. This particular Sunday he announced his intention of playing a recording of music by a band of boy musicians accompanied by Highland pipers. The concert went well, but I was especially struck by one pipe tune played by some locals from Glen Evans of all places. I knew the tune, but I couldn't lay a name to it. At the end of the selection of recordings, the announcer read out the names of the tunes with the composers' names. The tune I couldn't name was entitled "Flory's Farewell to Algoma," written by Rob Roy McGregor. Not many snakes have a pipe tune named after them, and that's a fact.

THE
NAUGHTY LADY
OF SHADY LANE

IT WAS ON AN APRIL TUESDAY THAT I RECEIVED A letter from a well-meaning lady who was concerned for her neighbours' cattle. She had the feeling they were being neglected, especially on weekends. Not neglected by the neighbours. The neighbours themselves spent their winters in Florida, returning to Ontario in the spring. Their cattle, however, were cared for in the meantime by a young man who was a distant relative. She was doubtful of his responsibility, enough so to insist we have a look.

I telephoned to ask just what it was that concerned her. Were the cattle thin? I asked. No, not really. Were they short of water? No, there were several heated water bowls. Were calving cows getting into difficulty, perhaps? No, not that she or her husband had noticed. Did she think they had lice? Oh, she couldn't be sure of that at all. Well, did they need a vet? No. Something just wasn't right, that's all she could say. She added that she and her husband never saw anyone there on weekends. After some reflection, I decided to leave that complaint until Friday afternoon. It didn't sound urgent, though I believed it warranted attention.

Friday morning found me with a vet in an unbelievably dirty barn south of Kincardine, within a couple of driving hours from the letter writer's object of complaint. An OPP officer from the local detachment had called us in for this one. It was the old story of the city slicker who wanted to turn farmer—without the experience, without the capital, and without the intuition and energy. The result was that his pigs had starved while he had sat watching TV soap operas in his warm farmhouse.

Out of a herd of forty pigs, five of the biggest, most aggressive and best able to compete for food were fat. Of the others, nine wandered feebly and aimlessly around, and twenty-six lay dead. This was early spring, remember, and the smell was unbelievable.

"These nine that are starving will have to be put down," observed the vet, "and the big five had best be moved. I'll call Alec Findley, he'll do it."

The city farmer sat slumped in a corner of the barn, fingering his loose change nervously and looking bewildered. He even looked a bit resentful.

Without thinking very much about it, I made up a set of removal orders for the vet. These are the certificates, completed and signed by a licensed veterinarian, stating that for the good of an animal's health it needs to be removed from its present environment. I next made up a set stating that the animals were incapable of living thereafter without pain and suffering, and therefore should be destroyed. The veterinarian signed both sets. I took out my "humane killer" and rounded up the unfortunate nine.

Alec Findley, a big, gentle man, arrived just as I had sent pig number nine to its happy troughing ground. We loaded the five survivors onto our truck and sent them off to the Society's farm in West Gwillimbury.

I washed my hands under the tap and dried them with the towel I've learned from experience to carry in my tool kit. I climbed out of my coveralls and boots, rinsed the boots and put them away in my wagon. Then I took out my notebook. I gave the "legal owner" of this rural mess verbal notice of intended prosecution. He was white and shaky. I cautioned him, according to the Judges' Rules Number Five, and stood ready to take down any reply.

He said, "I'm sorry."

I turned and walked to my wagon. The dead-stock van from Burnsal drove in as I was driving out.

I arrived at my next stop, Shady Lane Farm, at about two o'clock. The steady drizzle that had heralded my day continued. The farm gate was closed and locked. I parked my wagon, turned off the wipers, pulled on the rubber boots again and climbed the gate. There was no one about, not even the inevitable long-haired, collie-crossbred farm dog.

"Anyone home?" I called out. There wasn't a sound. The only thing I had seen as I drove down Shady Lane was a beige car, a Camaro, driven by a red-haired female figure wearing dark glasses. There were wheel marks in the farmyard that were slowly filling with rain.

Getting no reply from inside the house, I set off for the barn. A number of Angus-Limousin steers looked back at me as I splashed through their field. They had patches of hair missing around their necks and they obviously had lice. Their condition barely matched the legal definition of distress. I went on to the barn to see what I could see.

The cattle there had hay piled high in their feed troughs. Water was readily available. Salt licks lay in the bedding area like large, square blue hailstones. The manure had been scraped away. Binder twine from the bales of hay was carefully stowed in an empty grain sack that did duty as a garbage bag. The place was so clean it squeaked. Next I looked at the cow-calf operation next door.

The nursing cows looked content. The small, chunky calves with their long, black eyelashes looked like plump, mischievous schoolkids on Hallowe'en. The calf creep was overflowing with calf-starter. The hay and grain hoppers were full. I walked slowly round the expecting cows, eyeballing them for imminent calving. The cows eyeballed me right back. There was nothing wrong here, either.

In the normal way of things, I wouldn't dream of going directly from the house of the person complained about to the complainant, but in this case, since no one was at home, I saw no reason for being delicate.

I walked past the well-kept grounds and gardens to the house next door. I rang the bell, feeling like an Avon salesperson as chimes sang "ting-tong." A trim, well-dressed woman answered the bell.

"Hullo, I'm from the Humane Society," I said. "I've come about the complaint you lodged with us."

"Complaint? Complaint? I never made any complaint! You are highly mistaken. Good day, sir!" She closed the door firmly on me.

Something was not right here, but I couldn't figure it out. Slowly I climbed in my wagon and drove away. I stopped at the first filling station I came to, for the Eagle was low on gas. As the owner filled my tank, washed my rear window and checked the oil, I asked him if he knew of a beige Camaro in the area, and anything of its owner.

"Yes," he said, "there's a young fellow down the road who has one. I see it once in a while."

"Have you seen him today?"

"No. Come to think of it, we only see him in the middle of the week."

I drove home, still uneasy.

Seven-thirty the following Monday morning found me parked on Shady Lane some distance down from the farm. I had taken my dog Bess with me. For her, happiness is fetching a thrown stick, and we were thus occupied for at least an hour. At about eight-thirty, the beige Camaro drove past us and I again glimpsed the red hair and dark glasses. I called Bess into the back of my Eagle wagon and followed. This time the farm gate was open, and there, parked in front of the farmhouse, was the beige Camaro.

"Anyone about?" I called.

There was no reply. I went up to the house. The main door was open. I pulled the screen door open and called again, "Anyone home?" There was no answer. I walked in.

I caught a whiff of perfume at the bottom of the stairs. There was no one on the ground floor. All was clean and tidy, neat as a pin. No dirty plates in the sink, no half-empty bottles of ale or anything else lying about. Not even cigarette butts in the ashtray on the kitchen counter. I heard Bess barking and turned to see what was bothering her. She was looking in the direction of the barn. I went outside and joined her. She promptly turned to me and barked again.

I began walking toward the barn, taking my time. Something was distinctly odd about the whole scene. As I opened the door to the indoor steer pen, again I caught a whiff of the same perfume. I looked down the length of the barn. The in-calf cows were all turned looking at the barn's side door. I ran back to the steer entrance. There, running across the yard, was my elusive, red-haired Camaro driver. I ran behind, gaining ground. She was tottering on her high-heeled shoes. I put my hand on the screen door just as she was about to pull it open.

"Just a minute, miss," I said. "I'm from the Humane Society and I'd like a word with you."

She turned to me, head down. Red-gold shoulder-length hair, long dangling earrings, a black leather coat with a fur collar, beige nylons and brown high-heeled shoes were all I could see. But I could sense fear, as Bess had.

"Do you look after these cattle?" I asked. She didn't look up, but I received a nod in reply. "Who cares for them on weekends?" Silence. "What is your name?" No answer. "Come along, there's nothing to worry about, nothing wrong with them. They're in excellent condition." There was a shuffle of high heels, but her face was still averted from me. "Very well, then," I said gently, "I'll have to find out one way or another." Leaving her at the door, I walked into the house and up the stairs. A bedroom door stood open. On a dressing table was a brown purse with a wallet protruding from it. I picked it up and opened the transparent window section that held the owner's driving licence. I was startled to hear a man's voice.

"Give me that!"

I looked up. There, in the doorway, was the red-haired woman.

The licence read, Colin Lockwood. I handed it over, and the slim hands with the long, red nails took it. The elegant leather coat had been removed to reveal a white ruffled blouse and black skirt. The person walked around to the other side of the bed, turned and faced me.

"I suppose I must explain."

When the red-gold wig was pulled off, a man's short haircut appeared beneath. The plainly female person turned into an ordinary man right before my eyes. The white blouse, brassiere, false breasts, pantyhose, pull-on girdle, slip and skirt were discarded. As he pulled the slip over his head, one of his false eyelashes caught in the lace trim. I was sufficiently confused.

He was a transvestite, he explained. Although male, he enjoyed dressing in female clothes and spent most weekends in Hamilton pretending to be a girl. I learned that his background included an M.A. in Social Science and that he had taught at a nearby high school until recently. The farm's owners, his aunt and uncle, went south every November, returning in mid-May the following year. He had told them his nerves were troubled and that his doctor had advised a temporary change of occupation. They had left him in charge of their farm. It had been a heaven-sent opportunity for him to indulge in his fetish, and he had done so successfully until now.

"What are you going to do?" he asked me after an awkward silence.

"Nothing," I replied.

"Nothing?"

"No. Why should I interfere with your life? The cattle are fat and well. They are supplied with two or three days' food. Just be careful you don't have difficult calving, that's all. And get some treatment for the cows that evidently have lice."

His face relaxed, a sigh of relief escaped him. He looked almost happy.

"You can come for tea anytime," he said. He started to say more, but I thanked him and left.

Down at the gas station I called our head office. May answered.

"Can you go to Jimmy Quirk's farm at Santwood?" she asked. "He's been thrown in the slammer again. His dog's in the house. The house is open, you have permission to go in."

I acknowledged and set off on the Santwood errand of mercy.

This farm, belonging to Jimmy the jail inmate, was a total contrast to the one I'd left at Shady Lane. Old cars lay abandoned at all points of the compass. Corroded car batteries, stripped-down engine blocks, and treadless old tires littered the footpath. Collapsing cartons of "forty-eight," with their returnable bottles, were stacked in every corner of the porch. They once had contained a product that "smiled along with you."

Jimmy's half-breed shepherd bitch bounded up to me as I opened the screen door. I slipped the lead on her and walked her to my car. Bess moved to the front passenger seat, a position she adores. The shepherd was installed in the back. A travelling cage, folded flat, served as a temporary divider between them.

I went back to check that no other animals were indoors or outside the house. Looking at the filth, disorder, broken furniture and empty bottles, to say nothing of the smell, I couldn't help but think of Charles Fairbanks' quotation: "Cleanliness is a great virtue, but when you can't find your books or papers, which you carefully arranged, it becomes a bore." Jimmy was obviously never bored. Come to think of it, neither am I—chasing pigs, dogs and transvestite farmers.

I drove to the Society's shelter on Albion Road, booked the shepherd bitch in with the evening staff and drove home for supper. The sun was going down behind the hills of Caledon, all red and pink. It was a fine spring evening. Tomorrow I was to visit that pony farm at Talisken. But tonight at least I was home in time for dinner.

THE
TIGER
MAN

I DIDN'T REALLY MEET PHILLIPO FOR A YEAR AFTER I became aware of him, or to be precise, his animals. But it was inevitable that one day we would set eyes on each other. As I look back on it, I think my first intimation of his presence, or the presence of someone who let his lion take a run in a park almost as if it were a retriever dog, occurred about nine one morning when the OPP corporal in charge at Ashville phoned me.

"We have a lion loose here," he said matter-of-factly. "It's chased a man and his dog. I've seen the tracks myself. Can you come down and tranquillize it?"

"Certainly," I said, "provided you have a vet standing by with the necessary drugs."

The corporal readily agreed to this stipulation. I began to load the Palmer-Capchur gun, dart box and equipment into my Eagle station wagon. The whole ensemble has been loaded so many times it practically jumps in of its own accord when the equipment cupboard is opened.

Just as I was about to leave, the phone rang again. I picked it up.

"Inspector Serge, OPP here," said a sharp voice. "Have you received a phone call respecting an alleged escaped lion in Ashville today?" I replied in the affirmative. "Well cancel, will you," snapped the voice. "It's not a lion, just a big sandy dog. No need for you to come." I acknowledged his call, rang off and put the equipment away for another day.

The office staff and I speculated on the origin of the call. Had the corporal really seen a lion? If he had, in a town like Ashville, better it were taken immediately, otherwise a small panic would occur. But apparently he hadn't seen a lion. Privately I wondered just what the inspector would write on the corporal's annual assessment, on account of his having "seen a lion" in a park.

Sometime after this, on a rainy Saturday morning, I received a telephone call from the regional police. This time a man was trapped in his car, which had struck a Hydro pole, doing extensive damage. In the rear of the damaged car were two tigers. I was only half awake. "Are you sure they are in the car and not in the tank?" I asked, remembering an advertising campaign.

"There's no doubt about it," said the heavy macho voice, unamused. "Will you come or shall we shoot them?"

I said I'd be there soon. The last thing I wanted was policemen trying to shoot tigers with handguns. Not only was such an action probably unnecessary, but handguns would be ineffective for the purpose.

Once again I loaded the equipment into my wagon and set off in the pouring rain. There's something mean about a rainy Saturday. That particular Saturday there was virtually no one on the road as I bowled along to Ballandaloch.

As I neared the hamlet it became apparent something was indeed amiss. Red, amber and blue flashing lights announced that the police, Hydro and road crew were all present. Finding an unused portion of roadside, I parked the wagon, pulled on my raincoat and went to see what the problem was. I walked almost to the centre of the road, but no farther.

Crashed against a Hydro pole, which was now leaning at a drunken angle, was a large, battered car. The man I came to know as Phillipo was cowering on the front seat, occasionally moaning, and bleeding profusely from his right ear. Snarling and spitting, a female tiger, a Bengal by her looks, crouched on the rear seat. Beside her, a leggy Siberian-hybrid male cub was adding his contribution to the confusion.

Spitting of a different sort came from the live Hydro wires arcing and writhing on the wet road. The air smelled of ozone and burnt metal. There was nothing much we could do until the power was disconnected. We waited, watching anxiously and hoping Phillipo would not be eaten by his passengers.

Finally, after a strained interval, the wires were silent and we judged it safe to approach the car. I had the vague idea of pulling the tigers out and into a crate of some sort, but two things became rapidly apparent: the larger tiger was too big to pull out safely and we had no crate to put her in even if we did pull her out. This being the case, I came to the conclusion it would be easier to remove the man than the animals.

"Have you an ambulance on standby?" I asked one policeman as I fetched my horse-loading rope and electric cattle prod.

He was busy writing in his notebook whatever interesting things policemen write on such occasions.

"No, should we?" he asked in all innocence. "Who for?"

"The driver of the car for one, and possibly me if things go wrong." He gulped and nodded. "I also need some help," I continued. "Can you or your colleague help me get the driver out before we attempt anything with the tigers?"

"I'll call the ambulance," he said promptly, crossing to his cruiser radio. "Hey, Chuck," he called to the younger officer, "help this guy, will you?"

Chuck was younger and more powerfully built, but nevertheless not keen when I told him the object of the exercise.

"I want you to pull hard on this rope when I tell you. You'll have to be quick or we may have the tiger loose."

"I think I'd best attend to the traffic," he said quickly, and walked back to the roadway.

As I stood coiling the rope outside the car, I smiled reassurance through the window at Phillipo within, and beckoned to the crew of the roads department.

"Can you chaps pull on this rope when I yell?" I asked.

"Sure, we're doing nothing here," muttered the foreman, obviously without a clue as to what I was about to attempt.

I had fashioned a bowline loop on the rope's end, and now I readied the electric prod in one hand, holding the noose in the other. Looking to see if the road crew were ready on the rope, I nodded to them, then slowly opened the car door on the side of the injured driver.

Phillipo was holding his damaged right ear and exclaiming something in Macedonian. The bigger tiger retreated to the farthest corner of the rear seat. She crouched with her ears flattened. Alongside, the cub imitated her. I dropped the noose over Phillipo's bleeding ear and upraised arm, tucking it snugly under his armpit. Waving the prod in the tigers' direction, I shouted, "Pull!" Phillipo popped out to my left. I slammed the car door.

The ambulance men had arrived by now. They trotted over with their stretcher and took Phillipo away to the regional hospital. Taking back my horse-loading rope, now soaked with Phillipo's blood, I passed it completely round the car and over the doors twice, hoping thereby to keep them firmly closed while the vehicle was being towed away.

Although there were two tow trucks hovering in hopes of picking up a tow job, neither driver would tow the car to my friendly game farm. "We're not licensed to tow out of the county," they explained.

Meanwhile I had been watching the larger tiger scratch the back out of the driver's seat. I was persuaded it might be best to expedite matters.

"Tow it to the police pound," I instructed another, more willing tow truck driver, who had providentially appeared.

En route to the pound I stopped at a farm to purchase two freshly killed chickens. The tow truck driver stopped and waited for me. Might as well fill their stomachs and occupy the tigers' minds while we move them. I slipped the chickens through an open corner vent window of the car, then returned to my wagon and we resumed our progress.

At the police pound the constable on duty took down the necessary particulars, but he stopped short of trying to open the car doors to take inventory. No one would steal the stereo from this car.

The constable was most interested in knowing when I would be removing the tigers. I told him I wasn't sure, but as soon as possible. He telephoned his sergeant. From the amount and variety of his facial expressions I guessed he was recounting the story and explaining the present situation.

Returning to me, he cleared his throat and said, "The sergeant says you have to remove the tigers now." The tow truck driver must have overheard. Suddenly he sped off down the road.

"Well, officer, kindly tell your sergeant I'll remove them as soon as I possibly can. The person who owns them also owns the car and is well aware of their habits. He won't mind waiting. He's in hospital, you see. The big one chewed on his ear."

The constable's face was a study in alarm. I was untying my rope from around the car doors while I spoke. The constable ran back to the phone.

As I was finishing stowing away my ropes, prod, gloves and raincoat, he scurried back to me. "The sergeant says remove them at once, or . . ."

"Or what?" I retorted. "The tow truck's gone. I haven't a crate. And I've no one to help me if I had."

I was interrupted. "He also says if you don't get them

out of here he'll bring down the .308 and blow them away."

I looked at him sternly. I was beginning to feel a bit of real anger.

"Then, Constable, you may tell your good sergeant that if he does something silly like that, he'll be charged by me under Section 401 of the Criminal Code with killing an animal kept for a lawful purpose. Also, he will be discharging a firearm in a built-up area, another offence, and your office will be aiding and abetting the offences. I'll be back presently. After noon." I strode briskly to my car to avoid any further exchange.

When I arrived, the staff of the emergency department at the local hospital were on the point of discharging Phillipo, complete with yards of bandage round his head and ear. We drove back to the tigers in my wagon. The constable was delighted to learn that the crashed car would run despite its frontal damage.

"It's all right to leave, eh?" wondered Phillipo.

"Sure, sure," encouraged the officer. He was quite willing to be rid of us.

Phillipo eased himself into his sadly wrecked car and drove slowly away. I followed him to the city limit, and there I left him to survive as best he could.

The next time we met was at the Society's head office. He arrived one summer afternoon like a proud father, wanting to show me the cub. The cub was only half grown, but in Phillipo's "new" smaller car he appeared even larger than he already was.

Before I could stop him, Phillipo opened a door and called the cub out. It ran round the car park. The office staff watching it through the window were having hysterics.

We had, at that time, a printer named Beresford, a happy, whistling, singing fellow. He had been in the shed, where we stored paper, when Phillipo arrived. Accordingly, he had no knowledge of the tiger's presence. As we watched, paralysis preventing any interference, Beresford emerged from the shed. He was carrying two armfuls of paper, legal-size sheets. He could see ahead over the paper but not, of course, immediately below his line of vision. He walked into the tiger, who sniffed him with interest.

Stopping, Beresford balanced on one foot while he prodded at the tiger experimentally with the other. Unable to understand what the obstacle was, he lowered the paper and looked down over it. As he did so, he found himself looking into the tiger's eyes at a distance of five inches. With a loud cry he threw up both hands. Twenty dollars' worth of printing stock fluttered in the breeze of the car park. Beresford was gone. His long, thin legs broke the eighty metre record as he streaked across the back garden. Our neighbour's neat privet hedge was no obstacle. Unable to clear it in a running jump, Beresford ran straight through. The cub galloped half-heartedly after him but stopped at the hedge. We saw Beresford only once more, when he came to collect his severance pay.

Phillipo was strictly forbidden to visit us with his tiger again.

After that episode, nothing much was heard of Phillipo for over a year. Then I received a letter from him. It was headed H. M. PRISON and read as follows:

> *Honoured Sir:*
>
> *I am asking you to look to mind my tigers as they are with Mr. Dylan Morgan of Blackfoot. He is feeding them to chickens but not putting eggs inside for them, which is good. But sir he is not picking up the sheet. At present I am prevented from this by being in prison. Soon I shall be out. I will make you a big donation for all your good works, troubles and worries.*
>
> > *Phillipo Chalanbures.*

Out of curiosity, I went to the Morgan property. It was a rundown farm kept by an expatriot Welshman who had agreed to board the tigers for a nominal cost provided

Phillipo went in and cleaned out weekly. The animals had a large chain-link pen, which they shared with a female lion owned by Mr. Morgan. The pens were cleaned with a pressure hose. The animals were fat and fit.

This almost ideal situation had two flaws. One was the gates, the hinges and locks of which were rusting off. The other was that Phillipo hadn't paid a cent of the expenses. At my suggestion the gates were all chained shut.

Three weeks later Phillipo ambled into our yard. He was clearly upset. The Welshman had taken out a lien on the tigers and forbidden Phillipo to enter the premises until he had cleared the debt.

"No, sir," Phillipo began explaining his predicament to me, "you see, sir, the unemployment men come. They say I can't work and draw unemployment. It was for my tigers, sir. They put me in prison. Now I go back to my old job."

"What is that?" I asked.

"I guard the rubbish, sir."

Phillipo, it seemed, had a live-in job on a landfill site. There was little I could advise Phillipo to do but to pay his bills. Mumbling sadly, he left.

A week later Mr. Morgan arrived at our offices. The tigers, he reported, had been stolen, together with his own lion. Phillipo was plainly to blame. The police were investigating, but he had little faith in their efforts. I thanked him for the information and he left.

At five minutes to five that afternoon, I was putting away some typing at head office when a telephone call came in for me. It was the friendly corporal of police from Ashville. I sat and listened. Phillipo had done it again.

It seemed he had acquired a decrepit and unlicensed furniture van. In it, he had loaded the tigers and Morgan's lion. Confident in his own driving ability, he had headed west along the Queen Elizabeth Way. His confidence in the vehicle, however, was not so well placed. Bits and pieces of exhaust system, mud flaps, body, fenders, all had rusted through, and much had broken away as he drove along the throughway. The front of the OPP cruiser was rust pitted from following him too closely.

When I arrived at the police detachment office, Phillipo was penitent, apologetic, tearful and eager to please. He would agree to anything. I seized the cats as Phillipo, now in custody for stealing them, was ordered to return to Blackfoot for a bail hearing. Before leaving with his escort, he was also charged with several breaches of the Highway Traffic Act. The furniture van, it emerged, had been "borrowed" from the garbage dump for ten dollars. Plainly, other heads would roll.

As I was leaving the detachment, a fussy-looking man of medium height entered. His manner was authoritative but somewhat querulous. The corporal introduced him to me as Inspector Serge.

"Ah, yes," I said, "you once called off a lion hunt that your corporal here started me on. He was right, you know. There really was a lion. The owner just left here. He traded the lion for a pregnant tiger. There she is, with the cub, in the remains of the furniture van." I pointed to the derelict in the car park.

Inspector Serge spluttered, choked and went red. Seizing his snap-brimmed trilby hat, he left the room. I grinned at the corporal. As we transferred the cats from the furniture van to the game farm's travelling wagon, I chanced to look back at the window of the detachment commander's office. Through it I could see my friend the corporal standing in front of the commander's desk. The commander had an open file in front of him. As I watched, he drew a typed, signed sheet of paper from the file and tore it up. The corporal smiled again. He had been vindicated at last.

One fall day a familiar battered small car rattled into the office driveway. In agricultural circles its colour would have been called "calf-scours yellow." In it sat Phillipo, beaming. Behind him, on the rear seat, crouched two half-grown female tigers.

"Hello, sir. You see my new tigers, yes?"

I groaned to myself and smiled weakly. Phillipo was back among us. His return was a guarantee against boredom, if I needed one. I smiled again, more warmly. I had to go to a meeting, I told him. It was true, too. "Yes, sir," he agreed. But it was good to see him. "Keep in touch, will you, Phillipo," I said. I had suddenly found in myself a warmth and kindliness toward this man who couldn't resist wild felines. Phillipo grinned, flashing teeth that would have shown up the inventory of Ft. Knox. That's when I made a mental note and repeated my injunction to keep in touch. This time I was totally sincere. If ever again I needed help with a big cat, Phillipo would be the first person I'd call.

LOST PROPERTY
AND THE
SPIDER BANDIT:
A TALE IN THREE PARTS

WHEN I WAS YOUNGER AND, I SOMETIMES THINK, A very much nicer person than I am now, I was for some years a constable, and later a sergeant, in Her Majesty's Metropolitan Police. My first station was Paddington Green. Later I served at Ealing, Staines and at that holy of holies, Scotland Yard. My reason for telling you this is so you'll believe me when I say that when assigned to work on the front desk, one of the gravest responsibilities a person has is the receipt and care of lost property.

Now, if the responsibility were for property found in the street, that in itself would be enough, but the responsibility also includes property found or left in hackney cabs. The cabby, according to the regulations, is supposed to examine the interior of his vehicle when a fare quits it, so that he can restore to the owner then and there the property left behind. In practice, he usually discovers the lost property after the fare has disappeared. He then brings it straight round to the nearest police station, because then, if the owner claims it, the cabby is entitled to a reward, which varies between ten and twenty-five percent of the value of the item recovered.

It's an odd fact, but in my day, apart from umbrellas, the thing people most often left behind in the cabs was their false teeth. It seemed people would sit down, tired, and remove either their shoes or their teeth. On arrival, after the fare was paid, they would very often leave one or the other behind in the cab, usually their teeth. Since Paddington Green was close to Paddington Station, where there was a large amount of cab traffic, we received our fair share of lost items.

I remember one elderly cabby who deposited a set of false teeth on the counter. "Ain't worth much," he said. "National Health."

"How can you tell?" I asked in my innocence.

"Ah!" he smiled. "See these crowns?" He whipped out his own set of teeth, upper and lower, and laid them alongside the ones on the counter to show me the inlaid silver crowns. "Cost ah packet, aah can tell ya."

He replaced his valuable dentures. I logged in the dentures he'd brought us and stored them with several other sets that grinned at me from their shelf in the lost property cabinet.

These memories of my "lost property" years hurried back to me when Stanley, our senior warden in Lakeland, called me about a lost property problem at a motel in his district. A guest had left behind a canary and two budgies, in cages, and no less than six chinchillas, also in cages. What should he do?

"Take them," I told him, "and log them in as animals surrendered. Keep them until claimed."

"Right," barked Stanley, who is a man of few words.

Three weeks later Stanley telephoned again. This time he wanted disposal instructions, as the birds and beasts were still unclaimed. Local residents would be pleased to have the birds, he said. It was the chinchillas he was stuck with. No one wanted the six little furry creatures and Stanley did not want the chore of destroying them. I suspected that the owner hadn't either—he'd given a false address and car licence number. I said I would collect the chinchillas myself. Spring would not be long in coming and we were considering the opening of a children's petting park on our farm. The thought struck me that small, harmless little creatures like the "chins" might be just what we needed.

Upon meeting them I found these animals old and cranky. Furthermore, they had taken to tearing tufts of fur from each other. The male in particular could dish out a fair nip with his incisor teeth. Apart from their cuddly appearance, their only endearing trait was their way of leaping straight up every half hour or so and uttering an excited *"wheee!"*

The day I collected them was cold and everything that could go wrong did. For this reason it was six-thirty in the evening when I returned home, bringing the chinchillas with me. Since I couldn't leave them in my vehicle overnight, I put them in the basement on my workbench.

"Aren't they the sweetest things!" exclaimed my wife when I carried them in. Kirsty, our cairn terrier, whose special territory was the basement, had other ideas about them. These little grey critters would be something good to chew on if the varmints could be lured from their protective cages. However, she was so excited and set up such a crescendo of barking that she was brought back upstairs and locked in the bathroom, much to her disgust.

I had just sat down after supper to answer mail that was overdue for attention when the doorbell rang. It was my friend James, the vet. He had with him a small piglet that was recovering from a hernia operation. It belonged to a mutual acquaintance, Bill, a pig farmer who lived half a mile up the road from us. Bill and family were out for the evening at some farm function—would I mind very much caring for the little pig until Bill returned home, as James had to leave on what might be a long call? The pig was anesthetized and sleeping soundly. No, of course I wouldn't mind. I agreed to keep the pig till morning.

I picked up the scrubbed, white little piglet and bedded her down in a cardboard carton with some old newspapers. In a warm corner of the basement I surrounded her by a sort of pen made up from a metal fire screen, two spare wheels, tires from my car and four crates of empty bottles.

Once back upstairs, I enjoyed a cup of tea with my wife, watched the news on TV, and retired to bed. My daughter Kate came in half an hour later from a Pony Club meeting. On learning of the chinchillas and the pig she insisted on seeing them, and without consulting me she took Kirsty with her. Naturally the cairn burst into torrents of barking, aimed now not only at the chinchillas but also at the piglet.

The chinchillas all *wheee'd* together. Only the piglet was silent. I stamped out of bed in a temper to get things sorted out. Finally my wife soothed me, as usual, the dog went back to bathroom exile, and we all went to sleep.

At about three in the morning I was again aware something was wrong. Apparently Kirsty was still asleep, or if she was awake she was ignoring the noise, which was more than I could do. There was a second crash, followed by a clatter, then a new kind of clank, all from the basement. I got up and went downstairs. My wife helpfully let the terrier out to follow me, "for company," she explained later.

The cause, my soul, was the piglet. Recovered from the anesthetic, he was blundering around in the strange and lonely dark, bumping into all sorts of things. When Kirsty arrived she promptly began to chase it behind the empties, growling fiercely. Meanwhile the chinchillas *wheee'd* in full voice, evidently from sheer delight.

"The only thing to do is to take the piglet to Bill now," said my wife in what I thought was a very even temper for that hour of the night. I mumbled something about animals and trouble going together as I pulled on an old pair of navy blue serge trousers and my ex-British Army khaki pullover with the old shoulder patches. For some reason I still can't quite make out, I stuck my Irish thornproof hat on the back of my head.

With my felt-lined snow boots on my feet and the piglet tucked firmly under my left arm, I set off to walk the half mile to Bill's farm. I didn't want the piglet making a mess in my wagon. She could have travelled in her cardboard bedbox, but I just wasn't thinking right at that hour.

Songwriter John Denver has a line in his ditty "Grandma's Old Feather Bed" that says something about "six kids, three old dogs and a piggy-wig we stole from the shed . . . We didn't get much sleep, but we had a lot of fun in Grandma's old feather bed." I was striding along the main road, humming the tune to myself, when a police car stopped alongside me.

"Good morning," said the policeman, eyeing me speculatively. "Are you lost, sir?"

I assured him I knew exactly where I was.

He tried another tack. "Is that a pig you are carrying, sir?"

I agreed that what was under my arm was indeed a pig.

"Is it your pig?"

"No, it's not my pig."

"Well, sir, why are you walking up the main road at three-thirty a.m. with it under your arm?"

I was very tempted to say, "Because my name is Tom and I am the piper's son," but I refrained. I explained I had been pig-sitting and the sittee had become too much of a nuisance and was being taken home to its rightful owner. "Would you like a lift then?" he asked. I would, and climbed in, after he'd undone the all electric door locks.

We hadn't driven more than three minutes when what I had anticipated happened. The pig embarrassed me all over the bench seat. We suffered the smell in silence all the way to Bill's.

There was a light in the barn. Bill's son was dealing with a difficult farrowing. I handed the piglet over to him and, with a discarded grain bag, attempted to clean up the police car's front seat. Then I was driven home, where I tried to finish cleaning the mess with tomato juice and baking soda. The officer endured the whole thing with stoic patience. It was clear, though, that from now on his motto would be: "Let night-walking pig-carriers walk."

Next morning I succeeded in finding a home near Hamilton for the chinchillas and we had peace for three whole days.

The peace was breached by a call from a motel owner on the Trans-Canada highway near the Bay of Quinte. More lost property, I reflected as he explained that someone who had stayed in his motel had left four mink in one of the best rooms. They were in cages all right, but they smelled strongly and he needed the room. By telephone I requested the nearest warden to attend and remove the offending beasts. I would, I said, pick them up myself later in the day.

At that time I had under instruction a student inspector from a Caribbean Humane Society. His name was Winston, and he was a serious-minded young man. His present training included formal instruction, written assignments and accompanying one or another of us in our day-to-day work. He was a pleasant, good-natured fellow with a sleepy manner. Although mink are a scarce commodity in the tropics, they are fairly classic examples of the family Mustelidae, which includes weasels. I thought the experience would be good for Winston and accordingly I took him with me.

We went to the motel in question, where the manager showed me a registration card with an address in Lake Charles, Louisiana. I copied the details down in my notebook, including the car licence number. Next I checked with the local and provincial police to see if the owner of the mink might have been admitted to hospital, prison or mortuary, but nothing was known. I knew a mink farmer who would board the sleek animals until the owner could be located or we had to dispose of them if he or she could not.

We placed the mink in the back of my wagon in their double-lined crate, topped up their water supply and provided them with a tin of cat food, which they devoured with great relish. Checking to see that the two doors of the metal cage with its double-lined interior crate were secure, I closed the rear of the Eagle wagon and we drove off to see the friendly mink rancher.

For an hour, all went well. Winston entertained and instructed me, telling of his family back home and their donkeys. I in turn informed him about each breed of cattle and domestic animal in the fields we passed along the way. He had some difficulty in pronouncing the word "Simmental," the name of a breed of cattle then gaining popularity in south-central Ontario. Winston pronounced it "Simon tell." We had looked at several herds of "Simon tell" cows when I happened to use my rearview mirror to see what the mink were up to.

To my horror I saw that the crate doors were open. Two mink were loitering in the empty crate, but of the other pair there was no trace.

I stopped. Quickly. I knew mink were like ferrets, and ferrets have a quaint tendency to run up narrow openings like drains, pipes and trouser legs. I certainly didn't want a mink up my trouser leg, nor, I suspected, did Winston. Trying not to alarm him, I pointed out the empty cage and indicated the wisdom of our vacating the car, temporarily at least.

Slowly we wound down the two front door windows. First Winston, then I, wriggled through the open windows. I was able to extricate my heavy gloves from the rear compartment without permitting the mink to escape. I stood by the side of the 401 highway looking through the windows, wondering what to do next.

As I watched, one pair of mink wandered aimlessly over my recently vacated seat. Without really thinking I reached in through the still open window and grasped the larger one behind the neck. I went around the back and dropped it into the crate. Winston, ever keen to help, grasped the smaller female by the tail. Of course he was without gloves. She promptly ran up her own tail and bit Winston on the base of his thumb. "Eeech, damn, damn!" Though he cried out, he staunchly retained his hold on the animal. "Dis animal bite too much" was his brave complaint.

Using my gloves I hastily relieved him of the mink and thrust it in with its mate. Winston stood beside me slowly sucking the blood from his punctured hand and spitting it onto the road. "You see what I mean about their being fierce. Suppose one got up your trouser leg." The idea hadn't occurred to him before, but now it did, vividly. He went a funny leaf-grey and leaned against the car for support, a faraway look in his eyes.

"We must catch the other two before we can drive on." Winston nodded in reluctant but firm agreement. He was fully alert now. He wanted no more to do with mink and said so. Whether or not their next of kin were native to the Caribbean Islands was quite beside the point.

"Very well, then, I'll mind the mink. You walk down to the road to the next village, buy two tins of sardines and bring them back fast. It'll be dark soon." I handed him some money and watched him march off in his deliberate way. He was still sucking his thumb.

He returned forty minutes later carrying a rat trap. He also offered me a quarter-pound piece of pale yellow cheese, the anonymous mousetrap variety. They hadn't had the sardines, but when Winston had described his predicament, they had sold him these items. I noted he had nibbled the cheese on the return trip.

I couldn't use the rat trap on the mink. Their destiny had not yet been decided, and even if their demise was our eventual solution, it would not be by that means. Not wishing to waste more time, I fished my rubber overboots out of the rear of the luggage compartment, tucked my trouser bottoms securely into my socks, then zipped on the boots. There were no boots for Winston, but I was driving and needed to be reasonably safe—and not bitten below the belt, so to speak.

"Winston," I said, "you will have to ride with your feet up."

"I ride on de roof."

"Nonsense, you'll ride inside. You can wear my heavy gloves, that way you can catch the mink if they come anywhere near you."

Winston avowed he could stand being bitten in the hand if he had to, it was other parts of his anatomy he was worried about.

Finally persuaded, he climbed gingerly into his seat, trousers in his socks, collar turned up. He sat with his large feet propped against the windshield, clutching a tightly rolled Society publication on public relations. I knew he meant to swat marauding mink with it should any appear. I hoped none would.

We travelled the next seventy miles in this fashion. Winston for once showed absolutely no indication of going to sleep.

At the mink ranch we removed anything from the vehicle that was not bolted down, except for the mink and their crate. In the process I found the spare keys I was sure my daughter had misplaced and a dollar eighteen in change. Finally we were ready.

We chased one of the roaming pair of mink into a hand-held net. The other popped up between the seats and was grasped expertly by the farmer. Both mink promptly settled into their new home with the pair that were already in the crate.

We failed to locate their owner. No reply was ever received from Lake Charles, so the two pairs of mink stayed on the farm. I had decided mink were definitely *persona non grata* in any petting zoo.

The events in the third part of this story occurred one rainy evening in a small town in ski country. On arriving home, I routinely rang our answering service. The answering service relayed a message for me to call the sheriff's department in that small town, "Immediately please . . . a very urgent situation."

A very nervous deputy sheriff answered my return call. It appeared that he and another deputy had gone to a certain motel to serve some maintenance papers on a resident there. The papers were a committal warrant for nonsupport, to be served should no money be forthcoming from the man at the motel, who owed a considerable amount to his estranged spouse.

When the deputies had entered the subject's room, said subject had picked up a glass case containing a very large, evil-looking spider and brandished it with a happy smile. He had then threatened to throw this unpleasant creature at them if they did not leave. Needless to say, they left—quickly. The machinery of a whole legal process had ground to a halt with the introduction of one spider. Our assistance was urgently required.

Since I was on call, I drove off into the rain. At least I'd once more got out of doing the dishes. Some forty minutes later I drove up to the motel forecourt. In addition to the sheriff's officers there were two police cars with four policemen and a detective. I splashed towards them as they sheltered from the downpour under the porch, their eyes on the closed door to Unit 2.

From this concentration on Unit 2, I gathered that our "Spiderman" was within. Talking to the anxious watchers I was amazed to learn that during the wait for me our Spiderman had gone out for a walk, carrying his spider with him, and had returned purposefully to his refuge, in spite of the official entourage that accompanied him back and forth. The sheriff's men had followed him out and back, at a discreet distance. Spiderman had walked into a milk store, where he had picked up two bottles of ginger ale, some peanuts, a bag of chips and a chocolate bar. When asked for payment, he had threatened to release Aggie, the spider. The police were called, whereupon they, the deputies, the junior store clerk, and one or two bystanders had done nothing but follow Spiderman back to his motel. The police had ordered him to stop, but he had simply laughed at them. "Go ahead, shoot," he had said, holding up the glass case. "When I fall, I break the case and Aggie gets out." The troubled officers had wisely decided to remain passive, having learned by radio that a "spider expert" was en route.

The motel operator was on the scene and upset. "What if the spider gets away?" he wailed. "Don't worry," the senior policeman said soothingly. "This gentleman here," he indicated me, "is an expert from the Humane Society. He'll know what to do." I smiled. Privately I wondered just what I could do, apart from dropping a housebrick on the insect. There were no housebricks in sight.

It turned out that one of the policemen knew Spiderman, having arrested him in the past for stealing laundry. He volunteered to try the diplomatic approach.

He knocked softly on the door. "Henry," he called, "it's me, Walt Skilling, let me in, eh. I'm getting wet out here!" The door opened a crack and a bleary blue eye assessed us all. "Hi, Walt, you can come in, but everyone else stays out." Walt gave me a reassuring smile and walked in. The door closed behind him. We waited several minutes, then Walt stuck his head out. "Sir, would you please come in and look at Henry's spider?" I squelched forward and stepped into the dark room.

Henry, our Spiderman, was behind the door. He quickly closed and locked it once I was inside. Then he turned on the lights.

I looked at him. He was a small, skinny, unshaven little man, three parts drunk. He sat on a battered easy chair and nursed Aggie in her glass case. He held a glass of the stolen ginger ale, apparently mixed with cheap rye (presumably paid for). Beside him, on a side table, stood the stolen potato chips.

While Henry nibbled on these, I looked around the room, which was furnished in contemporary flea market. I chose a chair. "Want a drink?" offered Henry sociably. He proferred an open bottle of "Old War Bonnet." I do not, as a rule, drink on duty, but it occurred to me that alcohol and spiders don't mix well. I've known some collectors who kill insects with alcohol. For present purposes I was content to reclassify spiders as insects, and the taxonomists could send me admonitory letters as they wished. I reasoned that if the spider were released, alcohol might not kill it, but it would certainly slow it down.

"Sure," I said, bringing Henry the largest glass I could find in the washroom. I held it out for my host, who poured a couple of fingers. "Want some pop?" He was very considerate. I helped myself to very little ginger ale, wanting to keep the mixture strong enough to impede Aggie if the necessity arose.

I took a small sip of the bilious green, fizzy mixture. I looked at Aggie and smacked my lips appreciatively.

"Well now, let me have a look at your tarantula," I suggested mildly.

"She's not really a tarantula," Henry confided. "She's a Hairy Mygalomorph."

I looked at the red-banded, hairy black body. A southern Californian type, or possibly from Mexico. Not deadly poisonous, I thought to myself, but certainly large enough to impress, perhaps poisonous enough to make one very sick if bitten. Aggie was almost two and a half inches across the body, the fluffy black hair making her seem bigger. The five-inch-long hairy legs made matters appear worse than they really were. All the same, Aggie was an evil-looking creature, dangerous or not, and I had no idea how dangerous.

"Can I put my hand in and stroke her," I asked, my voice warm with interest.

Henry was speechless. No one had ever before shown such positive interest in his pet.

"Oh, well—sure," he grinned, putting down his tumbler of rye and Dry. He turned and placed the crude terrarium on the chipped fake-wood side table. I stood up, my glass of almost neat rye in hand, as Henry removed the fitted mesh lid. Just as I was about to put my hand in and immobilize Aggie with my rye, there came a heavy knock on the door.

Henry snatched up the cage, with Aggie inside, and held it to his breast. "Who's there?" he shouted. Walt, his policeman friend, who had been taking an entirely passive interest in the action up to now, went promptly to the door.

"What is it?" he asked softly.

"There's a reporter here from Orillia who insists on seeing Henry," we heard one of the officers say. "He says he knows Henry."

"Maybe he does, but right now Henry is busy showing us his spider." Walt emphasized the *busy* and *showing*. "Tell him, 'later'."

The rain-soaked officer obviously gleaned the intelligence Walt wanted to impart to him, for he retired without another word.

Henry now placed the spider and case back on the table. "Tell you what, Walt," he grinned cheerily, "I'll give you five dollars if you'll put your hand right in front of Aggie!"

"No way, not me," Walt shot back. "Those things give me the creeps."

Henry chuckled. He slowly placed one hand inside the terrarium and began to caress the round, hairy back. "See? She loves me. You want to try, mister?" He looked at me.

"Aren't you going to bet me five dollars?" I asked.

"No, you likely know all about these critters."

He took a long drink as I slowly moved my right hand into the terrarium and towards Aggie. The spider ran backwards as my hand approached her until, tight in a corner of the glass case, she had no room to manoeuvre. She reared up on her hind legs and struck out at my hand with her front legs.

"Down girl," I said gently.

Henry was thunderstruck. "She's never done that before!"

With my left hand I took out a pencil from my coat pocket. I had long since put my glass down, but not far away. Holding the pencil by the point, I commenced to pass it back and forth above the spider's head. She struck at it twice, then seemed to hesitate. She must have concluded that the intruder had hard fingers, even if they were her favourite colour—banana. She crouched down rather tentatively and consented to the stroking of my pencil. Walt looked at me in utter disbelief and no little suspicion. I now had the spider held down by the pencil. Close at hand was a moth-eaten cushion.

I nodded my head at Walt, who leaped up, throwing his arms round Henry in a bear hug and pushing him to the door at the same time.

"Come on in, you guys," he yelled.

"Walt, you bastard!" screamed poor Henry.

I hastily clapped the cushion over the top of the terrarium, picked it up and removed it to the washroom, where I placed it in the empty bath.

When I looked out the door Henry the Spiderman was gone, although I could hear his muffled shouts and curses. A car door slammed. An engine started, then its sound diminished with distance, and finally there was silence.

Henry was committed to prison for twelve months. He asked for his pet while in prison. However, the warden, a sensible man, was having none of that. Eventually Henry, apparently having some faith in me, signed the spider over to the Society, and I found it a home in a well-run zoo that accommodated tarantulas—another motel room was out of the question.

GO FORTH
AND
MULTIPLY

I WAS SITTING IN THE HUMANE SOCIETY OFFICE ON A rainy Tuesday before Easter, pondering my slashed budget and general shortage of manpower, when the phone rang.

A cool but somewhat edgy voice said, "Hello, Cyril Alibaster here. I'm the deputy administrator for the Town of Ambridge. We have a rather bad dog problem and our local Humane Society can't cope."

"Well, Mr. Alibaster, I'm not in the dog-catching business, why bother me?"

"Yes, I know, but this is rather special and has been bothering us for some years. Look, we'll underwrite the cost. Come down and talk about it over lunch."

As it was Tuesday and two days to go to payday, I hastily accepted the lunch, if not yet the job.

Cyril Alibaster was a tall, slim, scholarly-looking man of middle age. He gave me the impression of being an ecclesiastic.

"Do sit down," he said, motioning me to a well-stuffed, tweed-upholstered chair. "We have in Ambridge a remarkable state of affairs. We have a woman who has literally scores of dogs. The by-law officer can't get anywhere with her. She chased the public health nurse with a bread knife and your local organization is a joke."

"Excuse me," I interjected, "we don't have a local Society. The people you're referring to are an unaffiliated group. No connection with us." He was referring to a rather disorganized group of cat fanciers who rather grandly called themselves a Humane Society.

"Oh," he stopped, somewhat crestfallen. "Then they're not your people at all?"

"No, no connection at all." People who go around calling themselves a Humane Society when they are not are a menace to all properly established Societies. When I found out for myself what his problem was, it became obvious our Society ought to have been called in long ago.

"In that case," sniffed Alibaster, "we had better see the woman's son and daughter. I do hope you can do something about the situation here."

After lunch, a rather sober affair, I interviewed the son and daughter. Their story, on first hearing, sounded a little far-fetched.

The son declared his mother had "thousands of dogs" in her house. "I don't like to go there no more. My dad don't neither. He just throws her fifteen dollars worth of stale bread a week." I gathered I was dealing with a very broken home.

The daughter was a little more explicit. "She lives with my sister. They had three dogs a couple of years back. Now heaven knows how many. The house smells awful. We can't go there anymore. She's very peculiar. Dad left her on account of the dogs. I think she has a lodger. The neighbours complain, but what can we do? If we had to sell the house we'd be in trouble. No one would buy it except for a dog kennel!"

Mr. Alibaster offered the information that the house was zoned "residential." And that *he* wouldn't grant her or anyone else a kennel licence.

"Oh?" I said. "Has she got a licence then?"

"Of course not," he replied, reddening. "We haven't given her one. We wouldn't. That's one reason why we've asked you here." There were better ones, as I was to discover.

Armed with what I had learned from the son and

daughter, I went before a justice of the peace, swore on my worn and trusty Gideon's Bible that there were grounds for believing animals were in distress, and prayed, therefore, that a warrant of search be granted. The J.P. ponderously affixed his signature. Now all we needed was a veterinarian, and perhaps the luxury of a policeman. With the aid of the efficient Mr. Alibaster, both were shortly on hand.

The vet was young, keen and earnest. The policeman was also young, but pale, nervous and obviously wishing he were away solving some deep, involved crime. I felt middle-aged. My arthritis was playing up.

Our little group of officialdom drove along the neat streets of Ambridge until we reached #129 Reserve Drive, a detached bungalow, unremarkable except perhaps for the fact that it appeared to be the smallest house in the neighbourhood.

As we mounted the three steps of the wooden porch, the smell of dog became ever more pungent and overpowering. A heavy knock on the door caused a veritable fortissimo of barks in all keys, major and minor. No other answer resulted. With me leading the way, we three trooped along the breezeway in the direction of the back door.

The back door was secure behind the locked fence gate. We looked at each other. Clearly it wasn't the vet's job to shin over the fence. The policeman seemed engrossed with the cloud formations. I would have to go over.

Managing to scale the rickety gate without leaving any clothing or breaking too much woodwork, I banged on the back door. The barking that resulted was incredible. It was deafening. It out-crescendoed the Boston Pops, the launching of the QE2 or the take-off of the Concorde. It was an assault on the eardrums. I looked through the grimy windows. A large number of dogs looked back at me. There were dogs wherever I looked, wall-to-wall dogs.

"What the hell do you think you're doing, mister?" asked a thin, piercing, reedy voice behind me.

I turned and looked. It was a small, grey-haired, wrinkled woman. Neither the vet nor the policeman had had the decency even to cough. The speaker held a ten-inch carving knife in her right hand.

"Ah, good afternoon, madam," I began. "I'm from the Humane Society. We've come about your fine dogs."

"Don't give me that crap," replied the elderly lady with the carving knife. "Get the hell away before I cut you."

I looked at the policeman, he looked at me and then at the carving knife. As I climbed back over the gate I didn't take my eyes off the knife. She turned and scuttled back up the alley. We heard the door slam. The thunder of barking continued unabated.

Back on the street, I pounded on the front door again. A muffled voice within screamed something ending with "off." Tiring of the charade, I gave the door a good kick, and it burst open. Before the crone within could speak, I pushed inside. The vet and the reluctant policeman followed me.

Gagool, for that is what I was privately calling our charming chatelaine, started screaming abuse above the barking and yelping of some forty-odd small dogs that ran around the living room. She still flourished the carving knife. I took it from her, pushed it between the door and the frame and bent it till it broke. The pointed front half of the blade was stuck in the doorjamb, the handle half fell to the filthy floor. Turning to the vet, I motioned him into the centre of the room. "We can go to work now without fear of being wounded," I said cheerfully.

A pair of chihuahua-crossed beagles nibbled at my ankles. "How many can you count?" I asked. The dogs were trotting around all over the newspapers that covered the floor of the room. Eventually we agreed there were forty-three dogs in the living room.

A loud and persistent barking had been coming from the kitchen all this time. We wondered what we'd find there. We made toward the door. "Don't open that door," roared Gagool. "Don't open that door!"

The vet gave her a pained look. I gave her what I hoped

was a withering look. I glanced round at the policeman and noted he was pale, sweating and quietly retching. The ninety-degree temperature, coupled with the sense-defeating aroma of dog and dog droppings, had got to him.

We opened the door some three inches, and a three-inch-wide column of dogs, eight-feet high, appeared before us, a kind of bizarre monument made of canine flesh. We slammed the door shut again.

"I said not to open that door," muttered Gagool.

"G-G-G-Gosh," shuddered the vet. "How many dogs do you think are in there?"

"I estimate sixty-two."

"Yes, that's about right," he agreed quickly. Too quickly, I thought. But I didn't want to open that door again either.

I turned to our hostess, who by now had been joined by a younger woman.

"Madam, you have got to get better kennelling than this. I am going to make this order, under the Prevention of Cruelty to Animals Act, that you provide better kennelling within seven days. Do you understand?"

The object of my attention opened and closed her toothless mouth once or twice, then said, "Yes, I'm getting a place in the country at the end of the month."

I wrote out the order in triplicate, handed the top copy to the lady of the doghouse, and we shuffled out over the feces-strewn newspapers.

The next Tuesday I assembled eight men in three trucks, while the Ambridge Council contributed two men and a three-ton box truck. We assembled the vehicles on the parking lot of a nearby hockey arena. As we did so, I noticed two television reporters with attendant cameramen standing on the footway outside the doghouse.

The vet arrived, and our friend the pale policeman. I began to wonder what he'd done to get this detail every time it came up. (Probably he'd once given the mayor a traffic ticket.) A crowd of spectators gathered on the other side of the street. The vet, the constable and I made our way without speaking, before all those eyes, to the door of the dog-infested dwelling. There was no traffic and everyone fell strangely quiet as we arrived at the door. I was reminded of the film *High Noon*.

My hollow knock produced the now familiar tirade of barks. Gagool opened the door. She peered at us, fingering a brand-new butcher's knife. I stepped over the threshold and this time the other two, praise be, followed me.

"Well, we're here again," I began. "You still seem to have all your dogs." She nodded her head. She looked very unhappy. "All right then, we'll have to take some away."

I walked to the door, stood outside and whistled. For a second or so the silence was undisturbed, and then from inside the house there sounded a screaming voice that could be heard for three blocks: "You rotten, thieving bastard!" The sound-recording technician with the TV crew went cross-eyed between his earphones.

The troops were lined up outside. Cages were stacked on the porch, ready. "All right," I shouted above the barking and cursing, "let's catch these dogs!"

We then proceeded to chase dogs over sofas, under chairs, on the television set, behind the drapes and under the carpet.

It took some forty-five minutes to clear the front room of small dogs. Then we opened the kitchen door. The dogs in the front room had been small and in good condition. The dogs in the kitchen were large and very ill. Here were the mangy, the starved, the blind, the deformed. They were on the stove, the fridge, in the cupboards, everywhere. While the others gathered them in, I toured the house. There were yet more dogs in the linen cupboard, under the beds, and in the clothes closet.

Finally, I invited the owner, who by now was hysterical, to select three to keep. Sobbing, swearing, irrational and rational by turns, she picked three of the smallest, *pregnant* bitches. I made out the necessary documents and, after a last look round at the overturned furniture, the cupboard doors hanging by single hinges, and the droppings, we departed, leaving the oppressive smell behind.

The TV reporters closed in on us. I gave them a short statement, and my convoy moved away.

Out of one small, three-bedroom bungalow I had removed one hundred and fifty-nine dogs. Three remained, pregnant.

In the few weeks following, I received many letters from the owner. The media telephoned me daily about the fate the Society would decree for the animals. Each time the owner wrote it seemed she was on the verge of acquiring her "place in the country." She was always just about to acquire that haven, real or imagined.

Sadly enough, ninety-three of the dogs had to be destroyed, most of them from among the dogs in the second room. The other sixty-six eventually were found homes.

I had almost forgotten this incident in Ambridge until one day when I was concluding some business in a regional police department, an inspector friend was reading a list of wanted persons. To my amazement I heard him read out the name of my dog lady. She was wanted for altering the number of a Wintario lottery ticket and attempting to claim a ten-thousand-dollar prize. No doubt she was still trying to buy her country home. I hope one day she finds it.

THE
HERMIT
OF
OAK TREE HILL

ALEXANDER ARRASPAS NEVSKY WAS BORN NEAR
Kiev in 1898, the son of a general in the service of the czar
of all the Russias. He was reared to be an officer in his
father's regiment, and he was hurried through military
academy in order to be commissioned as a lieutenant when
the German-Russian arms race escalated and resulted in
World War I.

Nevsky fought without distinction in the war and returned home to find Russia in chaos. In 1919 he was
twenty-one years old, six foot eight inches tall, and
weighed about two hundred pounds. Although athletic,
his pre-war boar hunts, riding breakfasts and other social
outings had ended with the October Revolution of the Bol-
sheviks of Odessa. With his father's White Russian
Guards, he had been hastily drafted to put down the insur-
gency. Alas, Czar Nicholas and his family were finally
captured and executed, and in the end, Alexander Arraspas Nevsky and many of his ilk were forced to flee their
country. He never saw any of his family again.

Nevsky lived in Poland and Hungary briefly, making a
precarious living as a tutor of officers' sons. By some mysterious route, he wound up in Shanghai. There he joined
the international peace-keeping force of the International
Zone, the Shanghai Police.

With his great strength and height he became a legend.

Sailors from Scandinavia, Holland and other maritime nations quickly learned to respect and avoid the Russian giant, "Igor the Terrible," as he was nicknamed.

By World War II he was forty-one years old. He was too old for combat but just right for intelligence services. An Australian officer recruited him and he was sent to Britain for training. Following that, he found himself in Sweden as a military observer on the Russian border. At the cessation of hostilities, Nevsky was pretty much a burned-out case. And by then the Russians knew him very well, too. Not only was he a survivor of the old pre-revolution days, but he was also an active worker against communism. Twice the Soviet NKVD attempted to kill him. Twice his great size and strength worked to save him. However, his usefulness in intelligence had ended.

Upon demobilization he applied, with countless others, for resettlement in a safe, secure country. He was landed at Halifax, Nova Scotia, with seven dollars in the pocket of his new overcoat. After several minor jobs he was selected as head guard at a Northern Ontario gold mine. He worked there, unmarried and abstemious, until 1963, when he retired on the Canadian Old Age Pension and his savings.

He then bought two hundred acres of swamp, hill and bush in Muskoka. He camped out until he had built himself a log house, where he lived and bred German shepherd dogs. At the start he bought two of the largest brood bitches he could find and mated them to the finest stud dog in Canada. The puppies grew into massive, intelligent dogs that were in demand as guard animals by just about everyone with a need for such. They became known as Russian Nevsky stock, or "Nevsky" for short.

And so, Alexander Arraspas Nevsky found a form of contentment. He lived for his dogs. He had bought his stud dog in the United States and named him Sasha. Sasha shared Nevsky's food, bed and just about his every waking hour. The two bitches, Ludmilla and Glinka, were close companions, though they tended to be distant when with a litter. But all in all, they were the old Russian's family and he their guardian.

If the snowmobile had never been invented, I doubt I would have this story to tell. But in the winter of 1976, when the snow was deep around Nevsky's domain, Oak Tree Hill was invaded one Sunday by a group of snowmobilers from Oshawa. I don't suppose they intended to upset anyone, but like many of their kind, they did not respect private property. They drove onto Nevsky's bush and along his trails until they arrived at his cabin. They peered in through the window.

The old man was dozing, smoking a pipe of tobacco, when his adult dogs rose up in a clamour, and he woke to find three helmeted, goggled faces looking threateningly and intrudingly through his living room window. His first thought, at seventy-eight years of age, was that the Reds had finally caught up with him. Seizing the largest weapon he had, a double-barrelled 12-gauge hammer-shotgun, he burst upon the interlopers with his dogs.

He was still six foot eight inches tall, but now he weighed two hundred and fifty pounds. His hair, grey and matted, stood up all round his head, and his grey beard reached halfway down his chest. Roaring the Russian equivalent of "Come out and fight, you pigs," he was quite a fearsome sight. Too much for the Oshawa snowmobilers.

As one man they ran, leaving their machines behind them. The dogs helped them along, bowling over a man here and there, ripping the quilted nylon suits, but always returning to the giant unkempt figure who commanded them in Russian. To say the snowmobilers were frightened out of their lace-up boots would be to present an ultraconservative picture. They were terrified.

The little group clustered together over the small hill behind the cabin and considered their situation at two p.m. They needed to retrieve their machines. Two of the bolder ones ventured forward, crawling on elbows and knees, but the Nevsky dogs sounded the alarm and the bearded old giant emerged from his warm cabin and discharged barrels of shot in the direction of the invaders.

"What do we do now?" asked the youngest snowmobiler.

"Let's wait until dark and then rush to get to our machines," said another.

"What if he comes out and gets us in the dark?" a third asked, worried.

That clinched it. They agreed it would be best to get help.

Abandoning their machines for the time being, they set off single file to walk through the two miles of bush and snow to county road twenty-two. They broke through the snowplow-piled edge of the road at five-thirty. Hitching a ride, they landed in Dorset at six p.m. There they telephoned the OPP.

It was eight in the cold, clear evening when two constables on OPP snowmobiles roared up to Nevsky's cabin. His dogs warned him and he heard the engines before he saw the headlights weaving through the trees. He assumed it was more Soviet NKVD come to silence him. He wasted no time.

Lying flat on his porch, he steadied the sights of his .22 rabbit rifle on the headlight of the leading constable's machine. The first shot took the headlight right out of it. The rider hastily abandoned his seat and clung to his OPP comrade, who steered his own machine round and out of range.

Next morning, at first light, no less than twenty-two men rushed the cabin. They overpowered Nevsky, but only after three had been bitten by the dogs and two had received facial injuries from the old man's bony fists.

It was in the OPP lockup at Stormbridge that I met Nevsky. The police wanted the Humane Society to impound the dogs, partly because their owner was charged with one count of attempted murder and six counts of assault with a deadly weapon. There were other factors. He was also charged with harbouring a vicious dog, and there were the rabies quarantine regulations to be complied with. But was the old man upset by all this? Not one iota. He paced up and down like a large, hairy bear, snarling at his guards and demanding coffee constantly.

He calmed down when he heard me greet him in Russian. I explained I wanted to care for his dogs and that it would be easier if I knew their names, with a little information about their personalities thrown in. He listened gravely to my speech, nodding his great shaggy head in agreement, finally thanking me. I promised I would be back to tell him of my success, or lack of it, in collecting his dogs and bringing them to safety.

We were able to drive to the little cabin with ease, so many police vehicles had passed through the trail. The dogs met us, teeth bared, hackles up, defending their territory. Sasha, the male, was magnificent, and privately I admitted the courage of the OPP officers in not having shot the dogs in the course of their owner's arrest.

The two females were taken with little trouble. Glinka had two fat pups at her heels. Ludmilla had a swollen belly that foretold of another family in three or four weeks time. But Sasha was not to be caught. We tried to surround him, trap him, take him into the house. We loaded his food with sleeping pills, but to no avail. One agent lay prone on the porch, hoping the big black-and-gold dog would come over and sniff his arms. Despite the cold, young Bruce lay there for three hours as bait. And for three hours, Sasha stayed ten feet from him. It was a stalemate.

Finally, we decided we would visit the dog four or five times a week with food. Perhaps his insular mien would crumble a little, but whether it did or not, between our kibble and the rabbits he would run down, the big dog wouldn't go hungry.

The two females settled in at our Lakeland Animal Shelter, but they began to lose weight. In the course of two weeks, each had shed ten or twelve pounds, although they were fed more than our veterinarian thought they should be.

Helen, our supervisor at the Lakeland Shelter, had been thinking along with the rest of us. She said to me one day, "Do you suppose they miss not only the old man but being spoken to in Russian, as well?"

"My word," I replied. "Let's try it."

I went into the adopting wing and greeted the bitches in my halting Russian. Immediately they sat up, barked at me, eyes bright, tails wagging.

"That's it," exclaimed Helen. "We have to get some Russians to come and talk to them."

True to her word, Helen contacted the "Voice of Lakeland," the local FM radio station. For the radio people it was a great human-interest story. They said the dogs' owner was in hospital, which was true, since he'd been committed for thirty days for a psychiatric assessment.

From then on, at all hours, the Shelter was open, irrespective of regular duties, as Russian-born Canadians trooped through our door to bid the bitches "Strassvoitchaey." I was present one afternoon, just before closing. A large Russian lady had just bid the dogs a tearful farewell when a short, stocky man dressed in a black cloth coat and large, black trilby of the style favoured by Nikita Khrushchev arrived carrying a black leatherette instrument case.

"Good evening," he smiled with great deliberation. "I come sing for dogs, please."

He removed his hat and coat and hung them on the staff coat rack. From the underside of the music case he brought out a folding stool, which he pulled out to receive his weight. Taking a most magnificently inlaid balalaika from the case, he crossed one leg over the other, bent over the instrument and began to play. As he played, he sang in a fine, high, lyric tenor voice. He treated us to "Meadowlands," "A Beech Tree Stood in a Forest Tall," and the familiar "Kalinka." We clapped and cried, "More!" The dogs joined in, howling along in the higher passages, giving throaty rumbles in the lower chorus. He bowed, put away his instrument, closed up the seat, donned his coat

and hat, and left. He came every day after that, along with
the other Russians. It got to the point where, in the Shelter, at five p.m., between ten and twenty Russian-speaking
visitors would assemble, passing around cups of black tea
and applauding the singer, laughing and patting the dogs
when their canine voices joined in with him.

Nevsky's trial took place at the end of the month. He
pleaded guilty, explaining through his lawyers his mistaken impression of the trespassers and the two police officers. The judge placed him on probation and bound him
to keep the peace for two years. The officer's headlight was
mended nicely and the Oshawa snowmobilers moved their
excursions to Bancroft.

The old man was reunited with the two bitches at the
Shelter in a happy and moving scene. I drove him out to
his home, where Sasha had faithfully guarded the cabin all
spring, sleeping and sheltering under the porch and con-
suming the bagfuls of kibble we brought for him. The old
man, the bitches and Sasha fell upon one another. The
laughing, crying, barking, jumping, tail-wagging circle of
life and affection was one I shall never forget.

The Russian singer concluded his concerts when the
Nevsky bitches left the Shelter. It was a pity. We really
had been able to visualize the endless steppe country, see
the rivers Don, Dneiper, Lenn and Ob flow to the Arctic
Ocean, the taste of Russia caught in his rendering of great
folk songs.

I wonder what would happen if we ever had an old
Highlander come to entertain a kennel of Highland terriers in our Shelter. I have a feeling that even if the dogs
would not howl along with Angus and his bagpipes, the
cats just might.

THE
KING CITY
ROUNDUP

KING CITY, KETTLEBY AND SNOWBALL CORNERS ARE situated deep in the heart of Ontario's horse country. But don't think that only horse breeders, trainers and stablekeepers reside there. Oh no, the area is full of people who like residing in a horsey environment, on their two-acre lots with four bedroom, two-hundred-thousand-dollar homes. And here and there, tucked away up tree-fringed driveways, in modest houses, live descendants of some of the area's original settlers.

One such gentleman was David Churchman, a large, redheaded farmer who also doubled as plumber for the vicinity. His normal confident voice was highly troubled when he phoned me at my home. It seemed that in November of the previous year he had bought a small herd of Western crossbred beef calves from a drover. It was now July and time to ship the fattened steers to a Toronto packing house. The trouble was that two of them had refused to submit to shipment. At the first appearance of the cattle truck, they had cleared their four-foot fence in a manner that would not have disgraced a Liverpool horse. Now they were loose somewhere in the area and David feared they would cause some damage for which he might be liable.

I assured him I was prepared to help provided he hire a vet to prescribe and supply the drug for immobilizing the runaway steers. The drug would be run into the three-cubic-centimeter alloy dart that I would fire at the runaways with the Palmer-Capchur gun. He agreed, and at eight next morning we assembled on 17th Sideroad.

In fact, I had brought two guns, one that propelled darts by compressed air from a disposable cylinder, another that propelled the darts by means of a blank cartridge. I thought that the air gun would be quieter and cause less alarm, and I planned to use it first. As matters turned out, my forethought was of little importance. These steers ran no matter what.

We learned from David that during the night two steers had charged a motorcyclist, causing him to fall off his machine. No one had actually said they were David's steers, but we all knew they must be.

As we walked to the gate of the cornfield, a smart young lady mounted on a blood bay mare rode up and addressed us. "I say, if you're looking for those lunatic steers, I hope you catch them. They charged at Ryng Dove and me about seven this morning. Good job they didn't catch us. Ryng Dove's worth $40,000." David winced visibly at this last piece of intelligence.

We walked single file along the edge of the cornfield, David in front, me behind carrying the air gun, and James the vet lugging the heavy power gun and bringing up the rear. I was wearing my Stetson hat and carrying the rifle over my shoulder in a manner somewhat like that assumed by Robert Preston in a certain film of an Ernest Hemingway story. As I walked, I thought to myself that some people pay thousands of dollars to walk through steamy bush country just to have a shot at something. Here was I, complete with a gun bearer who was also a qualified vet, following my native (of Snowball Corners) tracker, and I was being paid for it. Sometimes life with the Humane Society seemed worth it. Here was a free safari.

My footsteps were interrupted by David's sudden halt. I walked into his sweat-soaked shirt and accidentally jabbed him in the rear with the rifle barrel.

"There they are," he whispered. I peered carefully around him and after some seconds made out two brown-and-white heads, complete with horns, looking in our direction. There was no breeze, so we had no need to worry about scent. We were better off than Hemingway's hunters ever were.

We put our heads together for a short conference. Ahead of us was an open gate, behind us a cornfield, to our right a hedge. It was agreed David would crawl through the hedge as a diversion and I would dart the beasts through the gateway as they watched him. David wriggled through the black-thorn, losing portions of his shirt as he went. James and I crept forward to the gate.

I raised the air-powered rifle and took aim at the first neck I could see. "Ready, James?" I asked. James held up the heavy power gun by way of reply. I squeezed off the shot.

The dart went to its mark with that soggy thwack that signals a shot gone home on any animal body. I had brought the air gun down and was in the process of exchanging rifles with James when several things happened at once.

The steer I'd hit charged forward at David, who jumped to his left, sideways, through the hedge at James and me. The second steer charged straight for the open gate, where we were exchanging rifles. I had a vivid impression of a large, heavy red beast very close to me and I seemed to be falling down. This impression was accompanied by a strong barnyard smell. James, I noted, had contrived to fall into the standing corn for a softer landing. That's what a college education will do for you. Just as I raised my head, David dashed through the hedge and fell on top of me. I was glad I was the one holding the still empty gun.

We gathered ourselves together and climbed to our feet. We were dusty, bruised and manure-stained but otherwise intact. We walked through the open gate and saw in the dew-wet grass the path taken by the dart-stricken steer. After circling the field twice we located the steer sleeping nicely under the hedge. We secured it with two ropes while David walked off to fetch his truck.

Our dozing steer woke up just as the truck arrived. A twenty-minute wrestling match followed—David, James, Bert the hired man and I versus the steer. Our tag team won, but only just.

We reasoned that if we stood on the roof of David's cab, we might see the second runaway making its way through the corn. David, James and I looked in all directions, but only a solitary groundhog rewarded our scrutiny of the landscape.

We drove along to the concession road, now something of a country lane with cornfields on our right and some exceedingly fine houses, complete with swimming pools on beautiful two-acre landscaped lots, on our left. We halted the truck and climbed onto the cab again. Off to our right a large body was moving through the corn towards the lane. It could only be the truant steer.

A nervous expectation seized each of us. I gripped the power rifle and noticed my knuckles were white. David stepped down.

"Listen," he croaked, his voice rough with adrenaline, "Bert and I will go into the corn and round him out to the edge of the road. You can dart him there and we can haul him right into the truck." Before I could say, "Go easy," they were into the corn.

As James and I watched the shadowy human figures among the green moving corn, larger movements rippled nearer to the roadway. The steer was coming out.

It was just then that a florid-complexioned fat lady wearing a track suit peddled her bicycle level with the steer as he broke from the corn. She was flattened on the roadside when the steer cleared the obstacle of body and bike.

James and I watched open-mouthed as the animal skirted a house and advanced at a line of laundry drying in the morning sun. Not slowing, the steer impaled a salmon-pink shorty nightie on one stubby horn and cantered onto the next lot accompanied by loud cries and curses, apparently from the owner of the nightie. That garment was now flying from his horn like a lady's favour on a tournament horse.

The next lot had a fine in-ground pool. In this pool sat its owner, on an inflatable floating seat. He was smoking a cigar and reading a copy of the *Financial Times*. His widely outstretched arms were holding out the paper, and his vision of the approaching steer was accordingly obscured. I think he must have heard the thud of a hoof a split second before the steer joined him in the pool. As the man dashed the newspaper and his ruined cigar onto the patio slabs, we noticed that the hitherto clear blue water was now a khaki brown. The dripping steer waded out at the shallow end and trotted into some bush that bordered on Keele Street.

We resumed pursuit, Bert and David clinging to the off-side of the truck, and simply shook our heads when the pool owner demanded, "Is that bloody thing yours?"

A tour of the area on David's semiretired workhorse yielded no further view of the runaway. We unloaded the one captive and tied him securely in the barn.

Over the incomparable Maritimer's tea provided by David's Nova Scotian wife, we discussed tactics for use the next day. The unseated motorcycle and bicycle riders weighed heavily on David's mind. As he spoke, he rifled through his portfolio of insurance policies.

"Perhaps I can get Bill Speers to fly his plane over to spot the steer," he suggested. This seemed a good idea.

We agreed we would meet at David's farm at eight in the morning. The plane would fly over, David would prevail on his son's Boy Scout troop to act as beaters, and hopefully the second runaway would be caught. Number-one escapee, now confined in the barn, was bawling his displeasure mightily.

Next morning it was raining. Nonetheless, half a dozen dripping, diminutive Boy Scouts waited at the end of David's farm drive. The low cloud and rain precluded any flying, so that idea was scrapped. James and I were waiting in his four-wheel-drive truck when David came out. It was clear he was still very worried.

"I'm sorry, fellahs," he apologized as he walked up to us, "but I can't see us doing much this morning. Maybe it'll let up by noon."

The Scouts trooped off. We were without our reconnaissance and our beaters.

"I should check the one we darted yesterday," said James.

He climbed down from the truck and I followed him. We walked along to the barn and entered the yard. The main sliding door was open and we stood squarely in it. There was yesterday's captive, securely tied. And behind him, eyes rolling, nostrils flaring, was number-two runaway, breathing heavily and crouched ready to run. We retreated hastily, carefully closing the door, and feeling a combination of vast satisfaction and relief.

Back at the house we found David trying to explain to CTV and Global News camera teams that there would be no steer roundup till noon. I whispered to him, "It's in the barn!" and we took our leave. He brightened instantly and began to narrate for the media a thrilling tale of derring-do that bore some resemblance to the previous day's adventures.

As we drove along past the scene of yesterday's clothesline catastrophe, we noticed a Simpsons-Sears delivery crew unloading a new clothes dryer. It's an ill wind that steers no one some good.

HIPPIE BEEF

THE PHONE RANG ONE MORNING, AND THE CALLER, AN apartment supervisor, was beside himself with indignation. He demanded in broken English that we come to his apartment building forthwith to take away what he described as "a cow." We asked if he had called the Animal Control for the borough. He replied that he had, but that they wouldn't help at all since the "cow" was indoors and not a stray. Thoroughly confused, Stu and I drove to Shepherd Avenue, York borough, to unravel the mystery.

York borough is a melting pot of nationalities and a modern, progressive community, well ordered and generally well run. A cow on the loose didn't conform to its image. We passed through the gates of the twenty-storey building we'd been called to and parked my wagon in the area marked off neatly for visitors.

As we walked up to the entrance, I couldn't help noticing that a bed of geraniums on the south side of the building was unusually luxuriant, twice the size of the blooms at the front.

The supervisor of the block proved to be an immigrant from Yugoslavia, a Mr. Krejimar.

"Ahh, you come!" he greeted us happily. "Now you see something you not see before. We have dirty people here! We got their dirty cows too!"

He motioned us to the elevators. Together with Mr.

Krejimar's Yugoslavian wife and the Hungarian maintenance man, all speaking a mixture of English, Serbo-Cro-
atian and Romanisch, we ascended to the twentieth floor.

As we trooped down the corridor, I noticed a strong
barnyard smell. Mr. Krejimar fiddled with his pass key at
an apartment door, then flung it open with a flourish.
"Now you see the real thing," he exclaimed. The smell
was overpowering.

We entered the apartment, which, although not eligible
for the *Good Housekeeping* Seal of Approval for tidiness,
wasn't by any means filthy. But the door to the last bedroom was closed. When we opened it, there, deep in
manure, was a Holstein bull! He was a calf really, about
eight months old, horns growing and just starting to get
aggressive with strangers. Apart from a pail of clean water, a salt lick, hay and manure, there was nothing in the
room but a battered easy chair.

Looking out of the glass sliding door to the balcony, I
saw the luxuriant geranium beds below. Obviously, the
manure that had been dropped on them was responsible.
The bull regarded us with interest, mooing loudly. We
stood back from the manure and studied the situation.

"Please, you gotta do something!" Mr. Krejimar was
beginning a monologue of self-pity and injured innocence.
"How me gonna clean up all dis, sir? Whatta mess!"

"How is it you never noticed this before, Mr.
Krejimar?" I asked. "What about the tenants below?"

"But we think dat ceiling go brown with smoking. I
kept telling dem, 'Hey, you guys smoke too much. Leave
off some, eh!' Frankly, sir, I think dey smoke that stuff—
hash. We paint the ceiling once, then dey say da paint no
good, so I tell dem, 'You fellows paint it and bring me de
bill.' Dey paint it and two days it is brown again. Boy, I
tell you, if dey pay their rent be o.k., but dey don't pay
noting. Just lots o stuff dey smoking! An' on de floor!"

More or less trying to ignore this tirade, I considered
how to move the young bull by the safest means. I left
long-suffering Stu to play cowman and I found a phone.

Following a talk with our vet for the area, I drove down to see him and collected a hypodermic syringe containing the tranquillizer Rompun.

When I returned, Stu was listening to Mr. Krejimar's second installment. I handed him a cow halter and uncoiled my vet's lasso. We roped the beast, who backed into the cupboard doors, cracking the hinges off one door. "Hold this rope, please." I handed the end of my lasso to Mr. Krejimar and carefully injected the contents of the syringe into the bull's neck muscles.

We gave the drug seven minutes to take effect, then we opened all the necessary doors and arranged for the freight elevator to be on standby. We walked the bull out of the apartment and up the corridor. The bull's mooing caused apartment doors to open, only to close just as quickly when the bull drew level with the startled faces framed in the doorways.

We all squeezed into the elevator, except Mrs. Krejimar, who declined to join us. While we were descending, the bull christened the elevator with his own private essence and the atmosphere became somewhat thick. Finally, the elevator doors opened.

By now the bull was amiable and relaxed. He climbed willingly into the dog van that awaited him and up the three planks we had rigged, all without so much as a moo. Stu drove him to the farm at West Gwillimbury.

I returned to the apartment at five p.m., where I met the bull's owners. There were four of them, all art students. They told me they had gone to the Sales Barn one Saturday, just for something to do. "Napoleon" had been a sickly little "bobby" calf, lately parted from his dam. He was weak and dying. In a moment of pity they had bought him for five dollars and taken him home in their car. Bottle-feeding, bread and cake, care and conversation had done the rest. The battered armchair had been provided so that, taking turns, one of them could sit and talk to Napoleon nightly.

They agreed to sign the bull over to the Society. We kept

him until he was eighteen months old, when we loaned him to a dairy farmer as a clean-up bull, with the proviso that he be returned to us when he was no longer needed.

The students then pitched in and cleaned house by throwing all the manure out of the apartment, over the balcony and onto the flower beds.

Two months later, on late-night television news, I saw a happy Mr. Krejimar receiving a trophy from His Worship the Mayor for having the best apartment-house flower beds in the Greater Boroughs. I bet he hasn't told anyone the secret source of his fertilizer.

THE
GREAT KILLALOE
PIG FIGHT

ONE WARM SEPTEMBER DAY, STU AND I FOUND OUR-
selves driving through Algonquin Park to the village of
Whitney. I had received a reliable complaint that there
was a herd of pigs in a neglected state at a rural barn
nearby. I had asked the regional police to verify the facts
for me, and they had replied in some detail, their conclusion being that all was not well. The owner had disappeared following a dispute with a jealous husband, but his
pigs remained—evidently now our problem.

Following the directions given us by the police, Stu and
I took a dirt logging road that grew steadily more narrow
and forgotten as we ground our way in low gear along it.

We found the pigs in their barn. It was not so much a
barn as a cabin adapted somewhat to house the pigs. The
cabin's furniture was gone, but the tattered lace curtains
remained, blowing around windows whose panes had long
been broken.

We looked through one window at the thirty-one assorted pigs confined within the cabin. The inventory began
with one large black-and-white boar and three sows—
black, white, brown, and all hairy. Some had produced
litters in the past, now half grown, black, white and spotty.
But most of the pigs were small, squeaking weanlings.

The condition of the sows was poor. They were thin
from lack of feed, and dehydrated from lack of water and

suckling their small piglets. Plainly, they would have to be moved from this waterless housing. Some two hundred yards down the roadway was a small running creek. We decided that a drink of water was of first priority, so I unbolted the front door and we urged the pigs out onto the old logging road, herding them toward the water.

The pigs were co-operative enough until they reached the creek. There they drank the water—and also discovered the frogs, catching and chewing them with squealing glee. Some of the smaller pigs waded into the creek belly deep after the startled frogs, and two that were in danger of being washed away had to be rescued. Both Stu and I were wet to the knees.

Rescue completed, we sat on a log, removed our socks, squeezed them out and contemplated our soggy boots, all the while watching our thirty-one pigs. Pigs are naturally clean animals and great lovers of bathing. These were quite happy now.

"We need a truck and a trucker," I observed.

"Yes, but we won't find one who'll drive three miles up this road," said Stu.

"Well, I'd better do something about it," I replied, and leaving Stu to herd the swine I squelched my way to the car and bumped off towards the main road.

Consulting the yellow pages in a phone booth, I found three livestock truckers listed. When I telephoned, not one of them expressed any interest at all in the job. The receptionist at the last one I called was sympathetic, however, but had to decline on her boss's behalf. She suggested I ring a Mr. Cundy, who did small jobs. I wondered if small jobs included moving thirty-one pigs along a bush road to some main shelter.

Mr. Cundy sounded slightly drunk but keen to assist when I outlined the problem. He had a pickup truck with which he could transport two horses. We could use the horses to drive the pigs along the road to shelter.

"That's no problem, me boy!" he said when I described

the logging road. I told him where he would find us, and without further ado he rang off.

Some forty minutes later, a battered pickup truck weaved its way along the country road. Looking over the cab from the red-leaded plywood walls of the truck bed was a pair of bush horses, heavy crossbred Percherons, calm and phlegmatic. Thank God. I had been having horrid visions of Mr. Cundy's horses as excitable thoroughbreds.

Mr. Cundy slid to a halt on the gravel shoulder and tumbled out of the truck. "Good day, good day," he mumbled in greeting. "Have a drink." He produced a mickey of rye whisky from an inner pocket and proffered it. My cold feet prompted me to accept. I took a good pull on the raw spirit. Mr. Cundy drank the rest of the bottle.

"Ish no problem, no problem," he assured me grandly. He removed a bolted sheet of plywood from the rear of the truck, and by dropping the tailgate down, created an innovative ramp. The Percherons, Dolly and Crowder, didn't use it. They simply stand-jumped from the body of the truck, backwards. They were already wearing Western-type saddles. Two battered, cracked bridles were buckled round their necks. No tack at Crabbet Park had ever been maintained like this.

"Now josh you jump on," Mr. Cundy slurred, attempting as he spoke to raise his right leg high enough to reach the left stirrup, a feat which, if completed, would have resulted in his sitting backwards on the horse. After some minutes he stopped, sighed and sat down on the running board of the truck, still holding Dolly's reins. The mare, a sagacious beast, stood over him resignedly as he snored.

I tied the horses temporarily to a fence and, after pulling its driver inside onto the seat, moved the truck into the weedy parking lot of a derelict Baptist church nearby. Mr. Cundy slept on. Riding Dolly, I led Crowder along the bush road towards Stu and the herd of pigs.

Stu was sitting on a cut log in the centre of the road, flourishing a broken branch in an effort to persuade the pigs not to leave. The horses, unshod, walked so quietly I was behind him before he realized I had arrived.

"Mind the nags," I said as he swung the branch back.

"Oh, you've brought Secretariat," he replied, casting a doubting professional eye at the two spavined refugees from northern logging. Stu knows something about horses, but I'd no idea whether he could ride one, as it had never before been an issue. "Couldn't you have found something suitable for Woodbine? Those two will split us up the middle," he groaned, indicating the girth of the animals. As I fell over the side of Dolly's saddle to the ground, my pelvis shrieked in a silent agony of verification.

Stu is short, but by using the cut log as a mounting block, he scrambled aboard the sulky gelding, and by pulling the reins like the steering lines of a naval gig, he manoeuvred Crowder round in an experimental half-circle. After some moments, he decided he was in command and fit to ride.

I prodded the three sows out of the creek with Stu's branch. This tactic was successful in getting most of the pigs moving along the logging road.

"Get the boar, will you?" I shouted over my shoulder.

Stu rode up to the boar, which reacted by taking short, jumping stabs at the horse's legs. Stu soon overtook me, legs splayed out, elbows akimbo, the boar following him closely. Rather like the master and huntsmen, Stu, the pigs and I hacked our way to the sleeping Mr. Cundy.

He lay sprawled across the truck's seat, cowboy hat over his face, one foot in a cowboy boot poking through the open window of the door.

"Hey, Cundy," I called. "We're here. Give us a hand, eh?"

A loud snore was all I received in reply. I prodded him with my leafy branch. He mumbled, scratched himself and rolled over.

"He's spark out, Stu," I said, surveying the scene from the broad back of my horse. She was standing in the middle of the road, where we were surrounded by pigs. Stu was trying to listen to me, but as his horse wouldn't turn, he had to lend his ear over one shoulder.

As we two equestrians maintained a controlled halt with our herd milling around us, a convoy of cars came over the hill to our left. They all had their lights switched on. In the lead was a hearse. Immediately, we both began trying to move the pigs off the road. But no sooner had we started to do this than a second convoy of cars approached from our right. The two convoys met our herding party in the middle of the road.

The second set of new arrivals were members of an Italian wedding celebration bound for a reception in Killaloe. From the honking of horns, singing and general merriment, it was fairly obvious the party had already partaken liberally of bottled happiness. They came to a stop and at first simply gazed at the rather unusual scene. There was nothing else they could do.

By now the pigs had become curious about the vehicles. They crowded around the hearse, grunting and snuffling with interest. Perhaps we could have moved them without incident had the boar not decided to scratch his buttocks on the back bumper of the high, shiny black Cadillac. This was too much for the deceased's brother. A tall, bony Irishman of stern visage, he climbed slowly out of his old DeSoto, walked up behind the boar and kicked its rear with decision and authority.

The boar, with half a dozen of his progeny, all screaming with rage and sympathy, scampered off down the road towards the Italian wedding party. By this time, the bride, resplendent in white satin, the groom, in rented powder-blue formal attire, the bride's father and sundry other guests in various stages of intoxication had left their cars and had formed a staggering line across the road. The boar and his offspring went through them like a volley of bowling balls aimed at a collection of wobbly pins.

The bride was the first casualty. She was bowled over, a piece bitten out of her skirt by the boar. In trying to save his spouse, the groom was run completely over by two smaller pigs, who left trotter marks on his hired coat. The boar went on to topple the bride's father, while one of his smaller sons left his own personal calling card on the father's trouser leg. Some of the guests were also run down. Others jumped or fell into the ditch while dodging the pigs. Stu and I watched in awed silence.

One by one the members of the wedding party picked themselves up. The father wasted no time in affixing blame for his family's misfortunes. He seized at once upon the deceased's brother. He marched up to the brother, uttering curses as he went, and struck the Irishman on the jaw upon arrival. He then nursed his hand by thrusting it under his left armpit. Fist fights were evidently a rarity for him.

The Irishman shook his head two or three times, as though he didn't believe himself. Then, grasping the father's collar with his left hand, he drove his right fist hard into the collar-framed face.

The air filled with Italian and Erse curses, shrieks and battle cries. The males first, and then the women, fell upon each other in the narrow, dusty roadway; a punching, kicking, swearing, stone-throwing, eye-gouging riot of humanity.

When Mr. Cundy awoke, he was entranced by the sideshow before him.

"Come on," I said to him, "you've slept long enough. We need help now."

We hastily shepherded the horses, sows and nearer pigs onto his truck. By skirting the funeral procession, we managed to get them clear of the war zone. The boar and his group of piglets would have to wait until hostilities ceased.

Stu and I did manage to round up the remainder of the male pigs, including the big boar, but not until two days later. They virtually surrendered themselves to another truck containing two young, squealing sows. Plainly, love was in store for them in our shelter.

Of the funeral and wedding parties, there was no trace, apart from blood-soaked tissue on the roadside and a muddy blue-velvet bow tie. The local paper had the last word. In reporting the deceased's funeral, it stated that the funeral cortege had been held up a full half-hour while the road was cleared of a band of wild pigs on a rampage. In the course of assisting the Humane authorities, several of the funeral party had sustained minor injuries.

I never did find out what the wedding party claimed. But I hope the happy couple's wedding album is desirably complete, pigs and all.

A HORSE
OF A
DIFFERENT
COLOUR

Hast thou given the horse strength?
Hast thou clothed his neck with thunder?
Canst thou make him afraid as a grasshopper?
The glory of his nostrils is terrible.
He paweth in the valley, and rejoiceth in his strength:
He goeth on to meet the armed men . . .
He swalloweth the ground with fierceness and
rage: . . .
He saieth among the trumpets, Ha ha; and he smel-
leth the battle afar off,
The thunder of the captains, and the shouting.

Book of Job, Chapter 39, verses 19–25
Holy Bible
King James version, unrevised

PLAINLY JOB KNEW A THING OR TWO ABOUT HORSES. Had the Romans paid more attention to horses and cavalry, their empire might have lasted longer. As it was, the Romans had the misfortune to encounter Goth cavalry at Adrianople in 378. In the ensuing battle the Gothic cavalry not only rode through the Roman Army, they rode all over them. Until challenged by Swiss pikemen and English archers in the fourteenth century, heavy cavalry was the supreme engine of war in Europe.

It's not my purpose to trace the crucial role of cavalry in

the history of Europe, but rather to make it plain that an enraged or excited horse is a potentially lethal animal. Not many horses are mean or vicious by nature, but some of them, like some men, just glory in a damned good fight.

March is in a cold quarter and it was a bitter day late in the month when, in response to a call from a regional police force, Stu and I wheeled north up Highway 400 to a little hamlet aptly named Tranquillity. Tranquillity Farm was easily seen from the road. It had the largest buildings for miles around and, rumour had it, the largest debts. At the main gate was parked a police car and two plain vehicles.

"Good day, Mr. Hepworth," the constable greeted me. "I called you because the sheriff here has a problem." He indicated a tall, distinguished-looking man with a mass of curly grey hair.

"Good afternoon, Mr. Hepworth. I'm Stuart McLicket, sheriff for the judicial district."

Mr. McLicket then went on to explain that he had a writ of possession and foreclosure against the property. There was no trace of the occupants. At first, unable to find anyone home, he had supposed his task, while not pleasant, would be easy, but much to his dismay he found three English sheepdogs snapping at his heels. Even worse, there were thirty-five thoroughbred horses. Obviously, he could not give a clear title to the mortgaging bank without some further ado about the animals. Thus he had prevailed upon the police to call for the Society's assistance.

My first act was to eyeball the animals. I had to try to assess just what we had on our hands. There was no one on the property, the sheriff explained, except a girl groom.

"What is she doing?" I asked.

"I don't know," replied Sheriff McLicket.

"Why don't we find out?" I suggested.

"Good idea. We shall indeed. Mr. Kovacks!" he called to his assistant. "We are going to look at the horses. Man the gates."

Mr. Kovacks acknowledged he was now in charge, and the sheriff and I set out to see about the stables.

The horses were in good condition. Roughly half of them were pregnant broodmares. The remainder were yearlings, two-year-olds, several "ponies," or lead horses, and finally, in their separate barn, four stallions. The girl groom was a young woman who knew her job, but her job included feeding, cleaning and watering thirty-five horses. It was far too much for any one person.

"My first thought, Sheriff, is that we not remove the animals but rather 'seize them on site'."

"My goodness, you won't leave them here!" he exclaimed.

I pointed out that I had no way of telling what stages of pregnancy the various mares were in, and that moving them when any one of them could be almost full term was courting disaster. Leaving them there but with increased help and supervision was far safer.

"No," he replied. "I have to give clear title and possession. I can't do that with the horses here, even if they're 'seized on site.' It's too complicated. They'll have to go."

I looked at my watch. Three-forty on a fast-darkening March day.

"Not much time to start today. Better go at it first thing tomorrow morning," I declared.

"Very well," he agreed. "I'll leave two men here overnight. I'll pay the girl for today and tomorrow, but the horses have to move tomorrow."

This last was said in his most solemnly official tone. I nodded my head silently and went perforce to the sheriff's office to plan the move.

Monopolizing the sheriff's telephone for ninety minutes, I succeeded in procuring promises of two horse vans and towing vehicles for the next day and two men to help with the horses that night.

Back at Tranquillity Farm, I briefed the groom for the night's duties. The evening hay was duly distributed and water was hosed into pails. The sheriff, Stu and I left the groom and the two extra men to wait out the night.

En route, I stopped to see a veterinarian friend of mine who lived nearby. He greeted me with mild amusement. He knew my visit was not purely social. I explained that I would need a vet the next morning to supervise the loading and unloading of various ponies, more than a dozen pregnant mares and four stallions. I added that the stallions might very well need sedative injections for travelling purposes. He nodded.

"You're in luck," he said at the conclusion of my monologue, "I've just taken on a partner. She'll be glad to help." The partner was not there at the time but would be dispatched for nine in the morning. Feeling I'd covered all my bases, I continued home to supper and to tending my own animals.

Next day dawned cold and grey, with rain and sleet forecast for the afternoon. "Just what we all needed," I said to myself. I drove to Tranquillity Farm slowly and thoughtfully. When I arrived the vans were lined up on the side of the road. The diesel engines of the towing units were rumbling away as though impatient to be about their business. My crew assembled punctually at nine and Mr. Kovacks drove up with relief troops for his night guard. A teenage girl in a bright red sports car was parked on the opposite side of the road and studying the congregation with great interest. There was no sign of the partner-vet.

As we planned our movements and activities, I made a little sketch-map showing the locations of the various groups of horses. I thought it might come in handy should the proceedings become the subject of court action.

I decided it was time to get moving and walked across the road and once again knocked loudly on the house door. My card, inserted over the lock, remained at exactly the same angle I had left it. Plainly no one had been home, even if Mr. Kovack's guards had gone off for a hamburger or whatever for a few moments. Very well then, the horses and dogs should be removed. "Get to it," I told myself. I had a simple plan: easiest horses first, difficult ones later.

I sent one truck and two men to remove all the lead ponies but one. I thought we might just need one later (and I was right). By this time Stu had joined us. The other vehicle driver and helper joined Stu and me in removal of the dry mares. There was no trace of the groom, nor of the promised vet.

I saw the loaded trucks away to our holding farm and sat down to make notes. I had just about finished when a sheriff's officer trotted up.

"There's a young lady here to see you," he announced.

"No idea what she wants, have you?" I asked warily. He shook his head. I had an idea she might be a keen young reporter for the national newspaper, which I had heard was "doing a number" on the Humane Society.

I walked the three hundred yards to the guarded gate with as much authority in my step as I could muster. Young lady was the correct description. She looked about fifteen. My own daughter, nineteen, looked old enough to have been her babysitter.

"Yes, miss. Press statements later when we are finished, please," I said automatically.

She looked at me with deep, deep blue eyes and showed a dimple. She giggled, "Oh, I'm not a journalist. I'm Dr. Suthers, Janet Suthers. I'm the vet."

After a short silence, all I said was "Come in."

She was, I noticed, the girl who had been sitting in the red sports car, too shy to announce herself. Glancing at the road I saw the girl groom peddling up furiously on a push-bike. "Sorry I'm late, but my son had colic. He's all right now," she gasped. She wheeled her bike up to the house and leaned it against the now-empty dog kennel. I introduced Dr. Janet and walked back to the barns between the two young women. It was beginning to spit either rain or the promised sleet. I felt like Noah, six hundred years old and loading up animals. Always loading up the animals.

"Perhaps you'll look at the broodmares, Doctor," I said. Stu was discreetly silent, or perhaps struck dumb.

The young beauty nodded and smiled, showing her almost-perfect teeth. She walked down to the broodmare barn and through the rows of box stalls. She halted from time to time to check on particular animals. I watched her with interest.

"Most of the mares have still got stitches in," she told me. "They can't foal until the stitches are removed. I don't want to remove any unless it becomes necessary. None of them looks as if foaling is imminent. I think they could be moved."

I noted down the time she had examined the mares.

"Perhaps we should look at the yearlings and stallions."

She nodded agreement, Shirley Temple dimples showing.

The trucks were returning, so I sent her ahead while I directed them to the broodmare barn. When I caught up with Dr. Janet she was in the stallion barn. Her presence there was signalled by the stallions' screaming and roaring. The groom had given them their morning hay, but they resented the stranger and were telling the lady vet so in no uncertain terms.

The chief complainer was the "king" stallion, whose name was Pluvius, the groom told me. *By Jove!* I thought, *Pluvius!* He was a bay, sixteen hands three inches. A fine, proud horse, he ran across the front of his box, arching his handsome neck and grinding his teeth, snorting and roaring. It was an impressive scene. A somewhat lesser but still very fine stallion, Winter's Hedge, was light grey, with some of the most widely flaring nostrils I have ever seen or ever hope to see.

"Perhaps we should sedate them now," I suggested.

The doctor considered this idea, too. "We'll put some sedative in their food. It will be easier than hypos."

She fetched her bag while I looked for feed bowls. We mixed the yellow crystalline powder with the sweet feed I'd found in my general search. We then opened the stallion boxes, one at a time, thrusting a feed bowl in to the feeding area of each box. The roars from three of the stallions subsided into satisfied muffled grunts as they licked up the corn and molasses mixture. Pluvius was not so easily fooled. He sniffed the feed. Evidently detecting the drug concealed there, he promptly scattered the feed across the floor of his box.

"We'll have to needle him," Dr. Janet decided.

I had the distinct feeling that that might be easier said than done. A glance at Stu confirmed my doubt. He raised his eyebrows and was off rather quickly to look after the mares.

Before long Stu and the others just about had all the mares aboard the vehicles. I asked Stu to remain with me. If we had to deal forcibly with Pluvius, it would be as well to have an extra pair of hands.

I inspected the rotund females already aboard the horse transport. Some peevish snapping and stamping was to be expected, but on the whole I was pleased with what I saw of our progress. Since the sleet storms were rapidly approaching, I was concerned that we move as many animals as possible before the foul weather overtook us. Away went the transports, while Stu, our vet and myself remained to make what in military circles is called "an appreciation of the situation."

We were unanimous that Pluvius would be the last horse to leave, since it was from him that we anticipated the most trouble. That settled, we set about readying the yearlings.

Some had halters on, some not. By scrounging around the barns and tack room we found serviceable halters for all but two. Stu and I fished the garbage bag for discarded binder twine, and by plaiting three strands of binder twine onto some discarded metal hardware—rounds and buckles of old halters—we managed to produce headpieces that we believed would hold up for the trip to the holding farm, and perhaps for two or more days afterwards.

This task was just about ended when one of the sheriff's

men approached us, as they had been doing off and on. This time the errand was an order.

"The owner is here. You're wanted at the house."

I walked down to the large house, noting the leaden sky as I did so, and the black clouds scudding in from Georgian Bay.

"This is Mr. Wonderling," said the police sergeant. "He's the owner."

"Good morning, sir. I'm pleased you're here. I have some papers for you with respect to the seizure of your animals."

"Send 'em to my lawyer," Wonderling snapped.

"And who is he, please?" I asked.

"Sam Iggle."

He then gave a phone number, rapping it off so fast as to be nearly unintelligible, turned on his heel and stalked off. I had hardly had a chance to study the gentleman, but my impression of him did not make me happier about the task at hand or its legal aspects.

For a moment I had hoped that the rest of the horses could remain at least overnight, but Mr. Wonderling's departure left me no choice. Nevertheless, I made ready all the seizure papers, just in case Mr. Wonderling returned or Mr. Iggle presented himself.

The trucks returned and we commenced loading the yearlings. Most of them had been born on the farm and had never even seen a horse trailer. None had ever entered one before. We endeavoured to load one or two of the older horses first, to give the youngsters confidence, but inevitably the time came when physical force had to be used on the most skittish.

We rigged two loading ropes, one to each side of the trailer. All hands wore gloves. Each of the reluctant horses was led forward with a chain lead-shank passed through its mouth. The two loading ropes, each handled by a heavy man, were crossed behind each horse, above its hock but under its tail. The chain in the mouth would prevent rearing and would bite quickly on the upper gums if the horse ran back. Everyone else stood ready to link arms and push. Gradually the horses were manoeuvred into the travelling stalls.

Pluvius was watching all this, whinnying, screaming and continually calling to his herd, diminishing before his eyes. Each horse loaded had to be walked past Pluvius's stall. As each one passed him he dashed up and down the box, and he soon wore a trench in the dirt floor.

Controlling the young horses, who were wild-eyed, snorting and sweating, required a maximum of cool effort. They reared and lunged forward, occasionally striking out at whatever or whoever stood in front of them. Needless to say, none of us stood in front of any one of them any longer than necessary.

Another sheriff's man panted up to us during our catch-as-catch-can lunch.

"You're wanted on the phone," he gasped.

I trotted down the wet, sleet-laden gravel road to the house. Mr. Kovacks held out the wall phone to me.

"Hullo?" I said experimentally.

"One moment, please," said a prim female voice.

"Who's there?" roared an aggressive male.

"Hepworth," I said.

"Who are you?" roared the voice.

"If I have to tell you, sir, you've got the wrong number," I replied.

"Listen," said the speaker, "you're the guy who's taking the horses out of there, right?"

I agreed that that piece of work had been most of my day's business.

"Well stop. Right now," he said. "We've got an injunction from the Supreme Court."

"That's nice," I said. "And when will I be privileged to see a copy of this injunction?"

"Mr. Wonderling is on his way up to you right now."

"Aah," I said, "you must be Sam Iggle."

"Right," said the voice.

"Well, Mr. Iggle, what you say may be true, but until I

see that injunction, my intention is to carry on removing the horses."

"I'm telling you to stop now," growled the voice.

"Should have acted sooner and not got your clients into this mess," I said and put down the receiver.

I checked with the director, who was in for a change, informing him of the state of affairs. For once we were in complete agreement, and despite clucks and squawks of alarm from the sheriff's men, I announced my intention of removing every horse possible before the writ arrived, supposing it was going to. The dogs had gone early on. They now were doubtless bedded down in the warm and dry, crunching up protein courtesy of Flag Rendering or some similar company.

I had held back one old and reliable-looking horse to assist in loading Pluvius. He was an elderly gelding by the name of George. The last vehicle had arrived to take off Pluv, as we now called him, with George for company. George trotted into the double carrier as though he were off for a holiday in Florida. He stood in his stall, snorting and whickering for Pluv's company. *Now,* as the English comedian Charles Drake used to say, came "the moment of truft."

Stu and I opened the door to Pluvius's box. Dr. Janet stood ready with the syringe. Pluv noted the vet in her white coat—perhaps vets also carry some ethosol smell or other agent on them that people engaged in other facets of the animal business do not—whatever the cause, Pluv lashed out one long, elegant foreleg, which passed between Stu and me and fortunately was a foot short of the vet. It was, I thought, not malicious, but intended as a warning: "Stay away from me."

By interesting Pluv in a quarter pail of feed, we distracted his attention enough to snare his halter with our lead-shanks. Stu and I changed them slowly, passing one chain over his nose and one through his mouth. Carefully and calmly, we led him forward. Dr. Janet came behind, only to fall back as his rear legs signalled a "No-Go Zone."

Just as we cleared the shelter of the stables, the storm we had been racing struck. Moments ago there had been a gentle slope down to the tractor trailer. Now the driving sleet had made a glacier of it, inviting one, both or all three of us to fall. Stu moved. Pluvius moved. I moved. We repeated this all the way to the vehicle, only to have the stallion balk at the wooden ramp of the trailer, within which George awaited. By now, the main crew were back at the farm and bedding down the mares. The driver of the trailer, Stu, Dr. Janet and I were all that remained to load the troubled and troublesome horse.

The driver took one loading line and Dr. Janet the other, but as she didn't weigh more than one hundred and ten pounds, her contribution to the present operation was somewhat limited. Stu took his lead-shank off the horse and took over her line. Slowly Pluvius was edged forward in a common effort. We had his forefeet on the tailgate board, halfway up now, then finally his hind feet. I was in George's stall, adjoining the one intended for Pluvius. The rattle of hail and sleet on the van roof made communication a matter of lip reading, mind reading or bellowing. Since bellowing upsets any horse, we said little.

I was trying, ineffectively, to urge Pluvius on when, for some unaccountable reason, he stepped quite smartly into his stall. The driver, with practised ease, quickly fastened the breach chain to prevent a run-back, and Pluvius was at last in position to be moved from Tranquillity Farm.

Dr. Janet came in via the groom's door. She was, I noted, wiping three fingers of her right hand with tissue. My nose identified horse manure.

"Did you goose him?" I asked.

"Sure did," she smiled. "My Dad used to do it with his work horses. It's not very ladylike, but it works."

George the gelding, now stalled satisfactorily with Pluv, stamped his impatience. It was four-thirty in the afternoon, near the winter feeding time for horses. It was time to finish the move. But as we should have known by now, Pluv had other ideas.

Why? Who knows? Perhaps because he had a horse in the box with him who was much lower in pecking order—he had quite an ego. Whatever the cause, he now began to kick and stamp. The more noise he made, the more he stamped. Stu and I talked to him, stroked him, whispered to him, hissed at him. He tried to rear and lunge.

"It's only a matter of time before he has the van over," observed the driver.

"I'll give you some nails and you can make coffins for us all," Stu glowered at me.

I tried to hold the stallion down with the chain portion of the lead-shank. I was lifted right off my feet. Wild thoughts went through my head of a bell-ringer during a Canterbury Double Change, just before the "stop" on the bell breaks. On a down swing I managed to get my right arm completely round Pluv's head and pinched his nostrils with my left hand. Pluv retaliated by dropping to his knees and bashing me against the stall wall.

"Needle, Doc" was all I could gasp.

Praise be, that small lady wriggled under the partition and pressed the plunger. Pluv continued to use me as a carpet-beater for some moments, but finally relaxed, stretched out his neck and uttered a deep sigh. We propped up his head on half a bale of hay and made him as comfortable as possible, given the circumstances.

I picked myself up, a little shaky. My backbone and ribs felt as though an entire regiment of guards had trooped the colour over me. I stood bent over, gasping for breath. Pluvius slurped his tongue, once or twice regarding me in a speculative manner with one large brown eye. I could have sworn he was laughing and saying to himself, "Best two out of three falls."

On arrival at the farm all horses were properly bedded down inside, except Pluvius, who remained on the floor of the horse trailer.

"Let him lie there," I decided. "He'll get up when he's ready."

"But I have to get home for supper," the driver muttered. "Besides," he added, "it's my wife's karate night. She'll kill me if I'm not home."

"Bring her round here," I shouted, walking off. "She can go a couple of rounds with Pluv."

Dr. Janet and I inspected every horse we had removed that afternoon. I held my flashlight, minutely checking skin abrasions, sores, stitches and scratches. Stu sat on a box in the horse trailer, chewing on a large cream doughnut and listening to Pluv snore. Our inspection lasted until nine that evening.

By that time Pluv showed signs of waking, and we managed to get him to his feet. Apart from the caretaker and his wife, we were the only persons left on the farm. I dropped the ramp, caught the lead-shank thrown to me by Stu, and managed to steer the big thoroughbred—who was regaining fighting form—into the well-bedded box prepared for him. We checked his legs and knees. Two patches of skin were missing. Dr. Janet fished in her bag once again for aerosol dressing spray, tetanus injections and soothing ointment. Finally, we removed our lead-shank chains and turned to leave.

I felt Pluv's teeth starting to close on my buttocks and did a stand-jump through the door, out into the aisle of the box. Everyone laughed, including Pluvius I'm sure. When I finally sat down, carefully, to eat my warmed-over supper, it was ten-fifteen.

Next morning, at nine-twenty exactly, by special messenger I received notice of appeal concerning the seizure. I had expected it to come eventually, but for it to arrive at nine-twenty in the morning, someone had to be upset.

The hearing was set for later in the week. The sheriff, his deputy and myself attended. I was at some pains to point out that the last thing I wanted was the responsibility for 2.8 million dollars worth of racehorses. Our insurance agent wouldn't stand for it.

The appeal board upheld my action. They agreed with me that the horses should be returned to their respective owners, on proof of ownership, not to the Wonderlings. The "proof" was the certificate of registration issued by the Jockey Club. The decision was publicized by the media and horse owners came from all parts to claim their horses, pay their share of the costs and find other homes for their animals.

Pluvius's owner sent his head trainer to claim him. In a sneaky sort of way I was sorry to see him go, for we were friends by now. No longer the roaring, box-running terror, Pluv was friendly and glad to see me on visits, welcoming me with whickers of recognition and affection when I stopped to say hello. The trainer observed that in six years of having charge of the horse she had never seen him so well behaved.

"You can always bring him back if he reverts," I laughed, but in truth I said it somewhat wistfully and I meant it. I was sad to see him go.

Three or four horses a day left us. The barn was emptying.

One day, a very well-turned-out East Indian gentleman arrived. He was dressed in a fine Crombie-cloth overcoat and snow-white turban, and driving an equally white Lincoln.

"I have come to collect my racehorse," he announced in an impeccable Bombay-Welsh accent.

"Fine," I replied. "Which horse is that, please?"

"He is called, ah—Winter's Hedge, yes," replied Mr. Umdellah.

We walked down the concrete aisle to Winter's Hedge's box. There he was, a dappled grey stallion, sixteen one and a half hands. He was in fat shape and his grey coat was sleek and satiny.

"May I see your ownership papers please," I asked.

Mr. Umdellah produced an elegant calf-skin case. He brought out a large envelope. "Ah, yes, I am having them here. Yes, here it is, Winter's Hedge."

I glanced at the registration certificate, made out in the familiar delft-blue inkwork favoured by the Jockey Club: registration number, name, height, colour—bay. *Bay!* Mr. Umdellah's papers didn't match the horse he had come to claim.

I pulled Winter's Hedge out and tied his halter to the cross ties in the aisle. I turned back his top lip to read the tattoo I knew should be there. I could make out a two, a four, a three, or was it an eight?

"What is wrong?" asked Mr. Umdellah.

"Your papers don't match," I said over my shoulder as I checked the horse's teeth.

I pulled up the top lip again, and as I grasped the front of the bottom lip the lower jaw moved downwards. The dental star was clearly apparent in the central incisor teeth. The seven-year hook was present, somewhat worn, though not greatly. The tush was clear and distinct, Galvayne's groove had not yet appeared. Yes, the horse was eight years of age, right enough. It matched the birthdate given on the papers. But the colour!

"Well, what am I to do?" asked Mr. Umdellah, who seemed a trifle alarmed. "It is my horse, you understand. I bought him at the auction. He cost me a lot of money. Now you say his papers are no good. Chak!"

"I didn't say his papers were no good, I said they did not match the description of the horse. He's the wrong colour. His tattoo has faded. I'm sorry, the best thing to do is get the papers amended by the Jockey Club." I pointed at the address on the registration form.

"But that is in New York, America. I can't go all that way!"

"No," I agreed, "You may get them amended at the Canadian office. In any event, they will be able to assist you. But in all conscience I cannot return a horse that does not match its papers."

"Yes, yes, I see, hmmm," Mr. Umdellah subsided into a low rumble. He smiled, "I see what can be done." He beamed at me, walked to his magnificent car and drove away.

At one-thirty my office phone rang. It was a gentleman who said he was from the Jockey Club. He was phoning, he said, to assure me that it was quite all right to give Mr. Umdellah his horse back. It was, he said, just a simple mix-up of registration. That was all.

"I see," I replied carefully, "and can I quote you as the authority?"

"But of course."

"What is your name and phone number, please."

"Gregory Gotunchuk."

He gave a phone number, which on checking proved to be in the Danforth and Bloor area. That was funny. I thought the Jockey Club was out at Woodbine, in Rexdale. In fact I knew damned well it was.

As it happens, I know the manager of the Jockey Club in Canada. Moreover, I know his voice. I telephoned him.

"Hi, Jack," I said when his secretary put me through, "Have you got a chap working for you named Gotunchuk?"

"No way" was the sum of his reply. That clinched it. Winter's Hedge would be staying with us for the time being.

At five o'clock I went home, thinking I might as well eat supper on time when I could. I was just enjoying the dessert—raspberries frozen last summer and soft custard—when the phone rang. It was the farm's caretaker.

"Sorry to bother you," he said. "There's an Indian gentleman here with all his family. They say we have their horse and they want it. They have five hundred dollars with them. In cash."

"I'll come up," I said. My custard had turned crimson.

It was just starting to rain again as I climbed into my wagon and drove to the farm. The barn lights gleamed through the steady downpour. Sloshing my way to the entrance of the barn, I saw the Umdellah group standing outside the box occupied by Winter's Hedge. Mr. Umdellah was there. So was Mrs. Umdellah, senior, a second lady I took to be Mrs. Umdellah, junior, and four brown children between three and twelve years of age. There was also an elderly Indian couple, plus two younger men.

As I approached, the children burst into a chorus of tears.

"You see, it's like this," Mr. Umdellah declared, "the horse is the children's pet. They love him very much. They want him home."

"If you want him at home, why were you paying the Wonderlings four hundred dollars a month to board him at their farm?" I asked.

He smiled. "Well, you see, our landlord won't let us keep pets at present." I thought his answer a trifle glib. "Can I talk to you privately?" he asked in a hushed voice.

We walked down to the feed room.

"Why don't you take this money as a donation?" He flourished five one-hundred-dollar bills.

"Mr. Umdellah, I would be pleased to take the money and give you a receipt for tax purposes, but you must understand clearly: no correct papers, no horse. Donation or not."

We walked slowly back to the group. The children again began sobbing, as if on cue. Mr. Umdellah spoke to the group. The women responded in high-pitched cacophonous voices. From time to time their dark eyes flashed in my direction. Their expressions were not the friendliest I'd seen that day.

"We go now," Mr. Umdellah ordered when the family appeared to have exhausted all the arguments they could summon.

"I'm sorry," I offered. Pretty lame, I thought to myself. Those tears were real even if rehearsed.

Next day I telephoned the Jockey Club. Could they, I asked, tell me who had owned Winter's Hedge prior to the Umdellahs? I explained my dilemma. They promised to call me back when they had news. In the interim more horses were claimed by their lawful owners. Only Winter's

Hedge and the eleven horses owned by the Wonderlings themselves remained.

A day later Mr. Umdellah called in. It was now almost as if he were paying us his daily visit. He brought his father with him, together with their holy man. The holy man giggled a lot and assured me that Mr. Umdellah was a very fine man. I nodded in agreement but stuck to my conditions: correct papers or no horse.

The Jockey Club called back about four o'clock on Friday afternoon. Winter's Hedge had been born and bred in Maryland and exported to Canada for sale as a seven-year-old stallion. His record as a stakes winner was undistinguished, and despite his being a good-looking horse, he had little to commend him as a sire of racing stock.

"Where was he sold?" I inquired.

"We're not sure. It might have been a private deal following a yearling auction. The last one was at Fort Ontario last September."

I made phone calls to the track mentioned but without result. Everyone had gone for the day, which meant it would be next week before I'd have any news.

Purely on a hunch I drove out to the farm on Saturday afternoon. Sure enough, the entire tribe of Umdellahs were there. Following routine, all the children burst into tears at the sight of me. This time the women joined in.

"Mr. Umdellah," I asked, "do you by chance have a receipt for your payment when you bought your horse?"

"Oh, my goodness, yes!" he exclaimed, hope reviving in his eyes as he fished about in his beautiful briefcase. "Ah, yes, here it is, lot one-one-eight, seven thousand dollars, Printer's Ledge. What is a printer's ledge, please?" he enquired.

I took the receipt and looked at it incredulously. There it was, "Printer's Ledge!" That was the horse he had purchased. By some fluke or a piece of careless bookkeeping, he had been given the papers for a bay horse named Winter's Hedge, which sounded much the same when pronounced quickly. Fortunately, the receipt carried the correct name of the grey horse. With some enthusiasm I pointed this out to him.

"Oh my, what does that mean, please?"

"It means the horse you bought was Printer's Ledge, a grey horse, correct?"

"Yes, yes," he responded, "that is what I am telling you."

"Ah, but they gave you the ownership papers for Winter's Hedge instead of the correct ones. Back to the Jockey Club on Monday, eh?"

"Oh, yes, yes, my goodness, yes!" He turned to his family and broke into an excited torrent of Hindi, interrupted by flashes of a brilliant smile. The effect was amazing. The children all broke into timid little smiles and the remainder of the family thanked me.

By Tuesday morning the entire Umdellah clan were back at the farm to claim their horse. This time they were armed with correct papers. They cheerfully paid their share of removal and boarding costs. When I finally handed the stallion over to them, they broke into gleeful applause. I then had to watch them wait two hours for someone who had agreed to trailer their horse and reneged on the agreement. Finally, they set off rather wearily to walk the horse to Don Mills, the menfolk leading it in relays, the remainder all riding in the Lincoln, which drove slowly behind, emergency lights flashing.

Why would anyone want a stallion that was too old to race and no heck when it had raced, I wondered at some length. I was to find out.

Later that summer I was idly sitting watching the local TV news coverage when the announcer gave out the news that a large wedding had been solemnized at a local temple. I was amazed but pleased to see Printer's Ledge being led along by some of the Umdellahs, with the bridegroom sitting in the saddle.

The groom, however, did not look terribly happy. His clothes were a little dusty and his entire appearance was a bit dishevelled. The announcer explained that the bridegroom had never ridden a horse before and had fallen off several times en route to the ceremonies.

The next day a horse trailer arrived at the farm. With it was Mr. Umdellah. His son, he told me proudly, had had a proper marriage, complete with a ride upon a white horse to the festivities. Now, having no other marriageable sons, Mr. Umdellah no longer required the horse. Printer's Ledge was superfluous to his family's social needs. Would we please accept him as a donation? For a tax receipt, of course.

I was quite happy to have Printer's Ledge back in the barn. We later adopted him out to a very horsey family, who registered him as a sire of show hunters.

Before we adopted him out, I had toyed with the idea of keeping him just to hire to Indian weddings, Moslem funerals, as King Billy's mount in the Loyal Orange parade, or even as Lady Godiva's mount in some university jollification. But common sense prevailed. Stallions are unpredictable. Ask Job.

THE
NORTH YORK
LION

IT WAS ONE OF THOSE BRIGHT EARLY SUMMER DAYS, and I was strolling north up Yonge Street back to the office following a lunch at the Spotted Horse. I was full of good humour and at peace with everyone when I walked in. I had held the appointment of head inspector in the Ontario Humane Society for six weeks. Everything indicated the job was working out well for me.

"Mary Ann from North Gwillimbury is on the line for you," said Marge, our receptionist. "She says they have a problem with a lion, of all things."

A wild panic raced across my mind. It bloody well would rain on my parade.

I picked up the phone. "Yes, Mary Ann, what is it?" I asked. I was a wee bit more nervous than I hoped I sounded. This was my first lion.

"Chief, you'll never believe this, but we have a lion running loose up here—on a farm, where it's kept as a pet. Can you do something about it?"

I noted the name and numbers of farm, lot and concession road, and said I would be along.

"Oh good, I'll tell the police you'll be there soon," she said and rang off.

I sat in frozen dismay. Now what?

First things first. I would need some help. I asked Augusta to use the radio to call up two of our nearest inspectors and ask them to meet me at the "lion farm" location as described. I then decided I would need the tranquillizer gun and I rummaged through my new desk looking for keys to the locked cupboard. While doing this I racked my brains for the name of a veterinarian I could call upon to assist me. I found the Palmer-Capchur gun safe in its case, but there were precious few darts for delivering the drug to the lion.

I finally decided that Dr. Secombe, the Municipal Zoo vet, would know about lions.

"Dr. Secombe, good day. Hepworth, Humane Society, here. Look, I'm sorry to bother you, but we have this escaped lion. Can you, er, help?"

The doctor listened to my story. He would be delighted to help, he said, but alas he had a most important meeting to attend. He suggested a vet from a neighbouring zoo. "Good luck," he concluded cheerfully.

Feeling a trifle down by now, I dialled the next zoo's vet. After some moments, he took my call from the monkey house, where he was treating a chronic tail-biter.

"A lion, eh," he replied.

"I need some Kytemine to quieten it," I begged.

"Love to help but our monthly review starts in twenty minutes. Look, why don't you try Dr. Schwartz at Lonsdale, it's just down the road for him. Do that. Bye, good luck!"

Good luck again, I observed as I dialled Dr. Schwartz in Lonsdale. He was out on call, his receptionist told me, but she would page him immediately. In the interim, I packed up the gun and darts in their tackle box, along with heavy gloves. I had been thinking about catching lions, and now I added our heavy-duty fish-landing net. Normally it was used for netting geese and other large fowl.

At last the phone rang. I pounced on it.

"Is that Mr. Hepworth of the Humane Society?" asked a calm, level voice. "This is the *Vaughn Hill Courier,* Debbie Smith speaking. We have a report about a lion on the loose. I'd like some information about it."

In some haste, I said, "We have had reports of it, too, and we are now investigating. There will be a release when there is any news." Before she could ask any further questions I rang off.

I was in the Gents when Dr. Schwartz called. I ran back to my office stuffing my shirt into my trousers.

"Dr. Schwartz?" I gasped, seizing the receiver.

"Ya," responded a voice with a German accent.

"We have an escaped lion just south of you. Can you help?"

"Ah, zo, a lion, eh! No, I am sorry ve haf a meeting and I am late for already."

I wondered, were they all going to the same meeting? I could just imagine all the veterinarians in Southern Ontario having adopted the policy of calling a meeting on any notice of an escaped large animal. "Lion escaped, gentlemen. Call a meeting."

It was plain no vet experienced with large, wild animals was willing to help me with mine. Very well, then, *any* vet would have to serve. I gathered up my equipment. "I'm gone to the Pickering Clinic," I said as I shot through the doors.

The clinic was the director's pride and joy. Animal owners could have their pets attended to promptly at low cost. The veterinary staff were booked up days in advance, but at this point that didn't matter. I needed a vet—urgently. I charged into the clinic's reception area.

"Where are the doctors?" I demanded. The clerk dumbly pointed to the basement. I pounded down the stairs. Our senior vet, Peter, was just emerging from one of the three operating rooms with his technician. He was pulling off his cap and mask in that languid way that vets and surgeons have.

"Hi," I greeted him. "Have you got any Kytemine?"

"Sure," he said, indicating the well-stocked shelves of the dispensary. "What's up?"

"Good," I replied, ignoring the question. "Have you any in your bag?"

"Yes."

"Syringes?"

"Of course."

I grabbed his bag and steered him up the stairs. "I have an urgent case up the road and I want you to look at it. I appreciate it's getting near the end of your day, it's the same with me, but this cat needs us." I pushed him into my wagon and drove my captive vet north without further words.

Peter sprawled in the front passenger seat. "What's the problem with the cat?" he asked.

"It's loose," I replied.

"You mean its bowels are loose?"

I was silent.

He sat up and he lit a cigarette. "Do you mean to tell me you've virtually shanghaied me from my clinic because a cat is running around outside?"

"Yes," I said.

"Bloody hell, man, the director will be furious."

"Yes, I expect he will. You'll have to blame me."

He blew out a long plume of smoke. "Don't think I won't," he said, subsiding once more into the back of the seat.

By exceeding the speed limit, running two red lights and generally carving up the northbound traffic, I made good time to North Gwillimbury and hit the concession road first guess. We neared the farm. Peter sat up when he saw the police cars at the lane entrance, two Humane Society wagons in front of the house and several assorted vehicles that collectively spelled PRESS.

"Hey, just what cat is this?" he asked.

"It's a lion," I said mildly.

"And he's loose," Peter groaned. "Damned if I ever go off with you again."

"Oh, come on," I said. "He's a pet. He's probably only a little lion." Out of the corner of my eye I noticed he was looking at the farm's exit lanes.

Richard and B.J. were the two Humane Society inspectors who had arrived in answer to my call. They came up as I skidded to a halt.

"Glad *you're* here, Chief, this bunch here are real idiots. The lion is out back. He's killed a goat and he's eating it."

"Well, that'll slow him down, he won't be inclined to run." I deliberately did not enlarge on the subject. Lions disturbed on kills will run all right—right at whatever happens to disturb them.

A police sergeant walked up. He seemed a trifle irritated with me. "Look here," he grumbled, "we've been waiting for you to get here since one-thirty p.m. How long is it going to take you to catch this thing?" I looked at my watch. It was four-ten.

As I busied myself greasing the tranquillizer darts and loading the adapter, I asked the police sergeant how the lion had happened to escape. He explained that it had been a hot day and that some bricklayers, rebuilding the main farmhouse after a fire, had quenched their collective thirst with a case of beer over the noon break. They had been sitting around speculating on the reasons why anyone would keep a lion for a pet when one worker had bet another that he wouldn't dare go into the lion's den and pat him on the head. The others had enthusiastically placed wagers, and, at length, the bettors had removed the scant four inches of baling wire from the battered hasp that held the pen gate closed. The bricklayer had walked into the pen, which was located in a bulge in the wall, in the ruins of the barn. He was halfway along the length of the pen when the dozing lion woke up and saw him. The lion sat up and blinked. The bricklayer's nerve failed. He turned and ran. By the time he reached the gate he was running so fast that slamming it shut on his way past was out of the question. The lion, quite naturally, ran after the man and out of the pen. The drinking bricklayers, seeing this, dropped their beer cans and lunches and took refuge on the roof. There they argued about who should try to sneak off and call for help. After perching on the rafters for some forty minutes, the builders noticed the lion stalking the luckless goat. At this point the most athletic member of the group was deputed to go for help. Whether or not he was the best runner was debatable. It did seem true he was one of the two principals initially involved in the wager that had resulted in the release of the lion.

I cocked a sardonic eye at the bricklayers, now gaining courage and offering free advice from the safety of their cars. "That lot fit to drive?" I asked. The police sergeant went off to confer with his men, and I was left to my equipment and my exasperated veterinary friend. We loaded the darts with a combination of two drugs, one fast-acting, the other somewhat delayed and not likely to put too great a strain on the animal's circulation, heart and stomach. We felt this precaution necessary since he had been gorging himself all this while on the unfortunate goat.

We drove out back in Inspector B.J.'s van and pulled as close to the lion as we could. Peter quietly opened the side door about a foot and my dart thwacked home in the lion's right buttock from a distance of forty feet. Startled, the lion ran. Peter hastily slammed the door on my gun barrel as the lion bounded right past the van, through the hedge and into the next field.

Richard had already positioned himself in the adjoining field and was tracking the lion's progress through the grass from the roof of his Ford Pinto. We drove round in the van, cursing the rocks and boulders concealed in the long grass as we bumped and rolled over them. The bricklayers, unable to drive away just yet for fear of "blowing green" on the breathalyzer, decided to help with the roundup, although we did go to some pains to direct them elsewhere. The last thing I wanted was the lion stampeded into a bush lot, where he would sleep off the drugs in concealment, then, like as not, emerge in a bad temper looking for another meal.

The police were preventing most of the inebriated bricklayers from approaching, but a few of them were truly persistent. I leaned out of the open door of the van and gave them some good advice. "Keep back, you fellows. He's not properly doped yet. We have to shoot more darts. If you get too close you may be hit. In which case you'll sleep for a long time." They stopped, grinning and chattering to each other nervously.

By now we had readied Richard's tranquillizer gun. This was one of the compressed-air type powered by the "sparklet" bulbs used in seltzer bottles. They often had too much power in hot weather and too little in cold. I was not in favour of this weapon and just hoped it would serve its purpose on this occasion. We loaded both guns. Peter stood ready, syringe in hand. Richard and I braced ourselves in the open door of the van.

"On the count of three! One, two, three, *shoot!*"

Ffffap, thwack! The darts flew in the lion's direction in the chest-high grass. We watched anxiously as the lion continued to stroll slowly through the grass that was so much like his natural environment. After several steps more than we expected, he stopped. Then he went down. We waited perhaps twenty seconds and decided he was out.

I pulled on the heavy gloves, then flourishing the landing net rather like a butterfly collector, I ran up behind the lion and seized him by the root of his tail, lifting his hind legs off the ground. The bemused lion turned his head in a sleepy fashion to determine what was lifting up his hind end. Peter and Richard were almost level with me when I happened to glance to my right. There, lying flat in the grass, were the two tranquillizer darts we had just fired. I gulped, hard and slowly. The lion had received only the minor dose from the first shot.

"Peter, hurry up," I said. "If this tail breaks we're in trouble." Richard and the bricklayers went into reverse and took shelter. In a real sweat Peter hastily injected the contents of his syringe into the right buttock. He was, I noticed, absent-mindedly massaging the drug into the muscle just as though the patient was some expensive thoroughbred horse, instead of a two-year-old male African lion capable of inflicting lethal injuries to both of us.

My arms ached from holding up the hind legs, but in truth I was afraid to release my hold should he wake thoroughly, turn and bite me. Sweat poured, my mouth gaped, my chest wheezed, but some moments later, the wide yellow head dropped onto the broad paws. Finally Peter shouted to me, "I think it's O.K. to let him go now." I opened my fear-stiffened grip and the lion sprawled at my feet. As a precaution, B.J. put the landing net over the beast's head. I collapsed on the grass. Peter and B.J. rolled the lion onto his chest, head to one side. The unblinking yellow eyes stared ahead. Our lion was well and truly out.

By now the bricklayers had recovered their courage and were keen to help. "We'll put it in the van," they offered. One was for taking it home with him. I pulled myself together. "The lion will be leaving with *me,*" I said firmly, "in *my* wagon."

I handed B.J. the keys to the wagon and asked him to bring it to our location. Then I ordered the bricklayers to leave the animal alone. All but one stepped back. There's one in every barrel. This man patted the lion, picked up his head and talked to him.

"I won't tell you again, sir," I ordered. "Back off."

"No, he's a nice little pussy cat, he's nice."

I took out my notebook.

"What's your name and address?" I asked.

"What do you want to know for?" he replied.

"I want to know who to send the bill to for this little comedy, that's what for. Now then, what's your name?"

The bricklayer let the lion's head drop, stood up and walked quickly to his car.

The police suddenly woke up and stopped the happy lion fancier and his mates from driving away. "We'll have your driving licences, please." Crestfallen, the crew allowed their names and addresses to be recorded.

B.J. arrived with my Eagle wagon. We picked up "Wallace," as I had christened the lion, and placed him on the floor of the vehicle. Collecting the particulars of all involved from the police, I asked that they use their radio to arrange for a message to be telephoned to my home, as I was by now late for supper. I also asked that my wife and daughter be informed that I would arrive with a vet and a lion.

Twenty minutes later I swung into my driveway. My daughter Kate, then aged fifteen, came out. She was fascinated by the idea of a runaway lion and wanted to see the sleeping Wallace.

"I've had my supper, Dad. I'll stay and watch the lion."

"Good girl, you won't lose by it."

"Ah, but what will I gain?" she smiled. "Two dollars, maybe?"

"Perhaps."

Peter and I went inside, washed our hands and arrived at the supper table. My wife bustled up with lamb chops, green beans and new potatoes. "I've had mine," she said. "Where's the other chap?"

I noticed the table was laid for three. "What other chap, there's just the two of us."

"The police called and told Kate you were coming home with the vet and a Mr. Lyon."

"Ah, that Mr. Lyon, he's sleeping it off in the wagon," I laughed.

"Can't he come in?" she reproved me.

"No, he's got no manners anyway."

"Really, Don, I wish you'd tell me when we have guests. How many are there?"

I smiled at her. "Come look," I invited. We walked out to the patio and she peered into the wagon. "Oh, er, well," she said. We trooped back in. I heard her giggling in the kitchen, "Mr. Lyon, indeed!"

We were lingering over coffee when there came a knock on the door. My wife went to answer it.

A woman was distributing religious tracts required, she explained, to save us from the Wrath of God, which was due, according to her good book, at just about any minute.

We listened, my wife at the door, Peter and I at the dining table. The woman was just working up to her punch lines when my daughter ran to the door where my wife was charitably allowing the missionary to finish saying her piece. "Tell Dad his lion is waking up!" The missionary paused in mid-sentence and glanced over at my wagon. Wallace was sitting up, yawning and showing his four-inch canine teeth.

"Oh my, oh my," she exclaimed. She gathered up her plastic shopping bag of tracts, executed a sharp about-turn and exited down the garden path.

Peter examined Wallace and decided he was not yet due for a supplementary injection, so we climbed into the wagon and drove off, leaving my wife with the dishes again.

The gas gauge was getting low, so I decided to fill up three miles down the road, at a small store run by an elderly couple. The man, hose in hand, came out as we stopped.

"Fill her up?"

"Yes, please."

Peter went in to buy some candy for Kate. I stood up to stretch my legs. The pump attendant washed my windshield with his squeegee. Finishing that, he turned to the dirty rear window. The glass became transparent once more as he scraped off the paste of damp and dust. Just then Wallace executed another of his yawns, and this time he roared a little for good measure. The sleep had done him good. He looked and sounded terrific. The man stared wide-eyed and open-mouthed, turned and ran into the store, and bolted the door behind him. He ran so fast that he trampled the filling hose out of my wagon. Gas had run all over the forecourt before I could shut it off and walk up to the store with my credit card.

Peter was inside the store when the man came crashing in. The owner's wife, taking change for the candy, asked what in heaven had gotten into him. "There's a lion out there, that's what," he gasped. His wife fussed around the counter and peered through her gold-rimmed spectacles at Wallace.

"Land sakes, Henry!" she cried. "Just look at all that good gas you've wasted!"

"I don't care about that," yelled her enraged husband. "I'm not going to be chewed up at my own gas pump."

Peter observed that Wallace didn't eat people, only goats. He didn't know that the woman's pride and joy was a white Togganberg nanny who weeded the back garden for her.

"My god, poor Rosie!" exclaimed the woman. She disappeared and then reappeared, pulling poor puzzled Rosie into the shop through the back door.

With difficulty I prevailed upon them to let me in to sign a sales slip for the gas in the tank. We agreed on a dollar and a half for the spillage. I washed the car down with the man's hose and left him washing down the forecourt.

The rest of the excursion was fairly uneventful, apart from two erratic tractor-trailers on the westbound 401 highway, their respective drivers having caught sight of Wallace and lost concentration accordingly.

We finally handed Wallace over to our friend Phillip and his assistant George at their game farm.

I'll tell you what to do if someday you're bored and want some harmless fun. Get a big station wagon. Put a tranquillized lion in the back. Drive out to the forecourt of a country gas pump. Tell whoever comes out to fill her up. Then stand back and watch.

THE
EPIC OF
MUFFIN INLET

The section of the U.S. Labor Code covering union rules for actors states in part: "No animal used as a performer in a theatrical production, including film and television productions, shall be unduly worked, trained or handled, except within the accepted practices as set forth in the U.S. Humane Society Film Liason Office Rules. Where animals are used in productions outside the U.S., any U.S. actor has a right, and should see it enforced, that these standards in respect of animals are upheld, otherwise no certificate of release shall be granted for that particular production."

IT WAS WITH THE ABOVE PIECE OF VERBIAGE TURNING over in my mind that I boarded the Sunday-afternoon plane to Northern Ontario. I was to supervise the making of a film with several animals in it starting at eight a.m. Monday. My wife was upset because it meant Sunday alone. My teenage daughter, Kate, had taken our horse, Harvey, to a show and would not be home until around nine p.m. All in all, the U.S. actors' regulations were not among my top-ten priorities that Sunday afternoon as I was winged northward.

After the usual comedy of errors at the baggage pick-up, I hired a car and set out for my hotel. I was driving through the northwest edge of town when the sound of a fire engine's siren caused me to pull over to my right. Past me went one, two, three, four fire engines, followed by a salvage wagon, followed by not less than four OPP cruisers. Behind them came a rag-tag of cars that obviously held journalists, stringers and plain old hangers-on. The thought struck me that in a wild, windswept town like this, the calling out of just about every piece of fire equipment for miles around must mean that somewhere there was a hell of a fire. If that were so, there was a possibility that animals were involved. I followed the convoy.

We rattled over the railroad tracks, past the new-and-used car lots that tend to mark the approaches to northern Canadian civilization, and out onto the northwest trunk road. I soon realized that this was the road I would travel in the morning, since it went by Muffin Inlet, the chosen location for the film.

As we neared Muffin Inlet, it was obvious the problem was there. About twenty cars were parked on the roadside. The fire and police vehicles ground to a halt, imprisoning vehicles already parked on the verge. I found myself a hole well back, parked and walked three hundred yards. I was aware of the vastness of Canada's inland sea to my left as I trudged through the loose grey gravel somehow representative of that Sunday afternoon.

As I neared the centre of interest, I had yet to see or smell smoke. Walking towards the provincial park, I saw the tail end of a small airplane sticking up in the classic stance of a 1920s movie plane crash. But there was no smoke, no fire, no smell of aviation fuel or glycol or brake fluid, not one of the classic smells one associates with aircraft tragedy.

I walked up to one of several OPP officers detailed to keep the forty-strong crowd of onlookers back from the site.

"Excuse me," I began.

"Get back," he barked. "If the gas in that goes, we all may get it."

"Wouldn't it be practical to move your line out to the main road then?"

He eyed me suspiciously.

"May I ask what is the problem, officer?" I enquired.

He eyed me again. "You can see what it is. The plane's crashed."

"My name is Hepworth," I told him. "I'm from the Humane Society. Tomorrow a film is due to be made on this location. I have a feeling you've encountered a film prop."

Now he really scrutinized me. "A film prop. What film?"

"It's called *Fangs Across the North,* and shooting starts tomorrow, eight a.m., at Muffin Inlet."

"Come tell the corporal," he ordered tersely.

We walked towards the plane wreckage, which was stacked tail up with a small waterfall in the background. A highly photogenic site. The corporal was a thick-set, knock 'em down, drag 'em out, dreadnought type.

"This is Mr. Hepworth. He's from the Humane Society," the constable announced by way of introduction. The corporal squinted at me and was about to say something equally short when the constable continued, "He says he thinks this plane is something to do with a film someone's making."

The portable radio in the corporal's hand squawked to life. Its message was to the effect that a plane bearing the same serial number as the wreck had crashed on a private field in Grimsby the month before. As we stood there by the car, an official from the Department of Natural Resources arrived. "We know all about this. It's O.K. Didn't they tell you fellows?"

At eight a.m. next day, after a fine breakfast of corned beef hash and fried eggs, I was back at the park on Muffin Inlet. Yesterday's deserted shores now resembled a gypsy encampment. Cargo vans, a mobile kennel and a four-horse trailer spelled animals. Make-up artists scurried from one mobile home to another; film technicians bustled about with cans of film; carpenters, gaffers and others carried items of all kinds. A crew of men from the nearby Indian reservation had been hired as porters. They stolidly carried flood lights, camera tripods and other heavy items up a steep, narrow track to the crash site.

I stood there trying to make sense of the scene. As I watched the activity, a short, stout man with heavy horn-rim glasses, curly hair, an enormous moustache and bushy beard came up. He looked like a ship's worn-out cargo mat with glasses.

"Halloo," he greeted me cheerily. "I'm Myrvin Cohen, production manager. I take it you must be Mr. What's-his-name from the Humane Society." I agreed that was probably me. "Well," he went on, "we're not shooting any animals before lunchtime, so you can take off." I said, No. "Of course you're welcome to stay," he added hastily.

I stayed. Finding the canteen wagon, I sipped the film company's bitter coffee and continued studying the scene.

A tall man, strikingly handsome, wearing a plaid shirt, khaki pants and bush boots, strode up and smiled at me. "Hi," he purred. "I'm Neville Dent." I told him I was delighted to know that. Mr. Dent then proceeded to tell me what a difficult time he had endured as an actor. I hmm-hmm'd in sympathy. "You're from the local TV station?" he asked. I said no, I was from Toronto, and at that he positively warmed to me. "Why don't you come to our party tonight," he pleaded. I said I'd be pleased to look in. He laid a friendly hand on my shoulder. "I'm so glad we met," he gushed. I was saying something suitable in reply but was interrupted. One of the stout, battered-looking ladies who manned the mobile home ticketed MALE MAKE-UP had her head stuck out of its door. "Dent, Dent!" she screamed, "NOW." My new chum smiled. "That's me, I'm due in make-up." He trotted up to the trailer. The formidable female in the door said, loudly enough for me to hear, "Get in there, you worm. Sit in that there chair and shut up." Mr. Dent smiled at me and hung his head like a schoolboy caught stealing apples.

During our brief conversation he had told me how, after four years of laying siege to every agent in Toronto, he had finally succeeded in obtaining a part in a real live film. He was "in make-up" some fifteen minutes. When he reappeared, his handsome face was a pallid white, his lips were grey. He looked like a corpse. I stared at him aghast.

"What part are you playing?" I asked.

"The dead pilot. It's a quiet part."

I nodded my head in agreement.

At ten a.m. I met the trainer, along with the bear and cougar that were cast in the production. The trainer, Fred, had but a hazy idea of what was required of him. I looked at the cougar. He was a two-year-old male just reaching puberty, a fact which to me spelled trouble. The bear was about fourteen months old, too young to know what was required of him. More trouble.

I conversed with the production manager between takes, and I learned the bear was to be used late in the morning. The script called for the bear to run up to the camera, then walk away. The bear was not trained to run up to anything, let alone a movie camera with arc lights. I had a feeling the bear might just walk up to the camera then run away—for good.

I spoke to Fred about it. He proposed to tranquillize the bear using a solution of nicotine sulphate. I was against that plan since this substance is a poison for which there is no antidote. It is always difficult to judge accurately, in the case of animals, how much of any drug to give, and overdosing is always a real possibility. It can be provided for only by having an antidote on hand. Fred then said he'd shoot the bear dead on conclusion of a successful take. This I also vetoed. I was beginning to see why I was needed.

"Why don't we have a vet?" I asked. "That would settle the whole question."

The production manager reacted as though I had asked him to donate a vital organ to a Third World country. "No budget!" he screamed.

"All right." I had an idea. "There are enough people here, we can surround the bear with a length of snow-fencing to funnel it back into its travelling crate."

This was agreed upon. Two lengths of snow-fencing were "borrowed" from the province's storage at the park entrance.

The time for the bear's "take" arrived. The camera was moved to the interior of a large travelling cage. This, I learned, was not to protect the cameraman, but to simulate the dog's-eye view of the approaching and departing bear. The dog was in a travelling cage because it had been thrown from the aircraft on impact when the plane crashed. Thus, the story went, the imprisoned dog is seen to be visited by a parade of wildlife before his release by a cougar who accidentally strikes the door catch.

The bear had been starved for two days. The reason for this was to make him likely to make a bee (or bear) line for some tempting fried chicken placed under the cage. The porters, labourers and any other hangers-on were strategically placed so as to close in on the bear and, with the aid of the snow fence, urge him back into his crate.

The production manager now began to follow me around like a puppy dog. I asked for more persons to be stationed near a bend in the little river. There, the clear, cold water rippled over a gravelled shallow where I guessed the bear would cross if he crossed at all. Some of the Indians were directed to stand on the bend. Two of them immediately waded to the far side, thereby putting the stream between themselves and the bear.

I stationed myself to the left side of the cameraman to head off the bear if he didn't stop to eat fried chicken. I replaced my stock cane with my electric cattle prod, a humane and useful defence against almost any animal. The production manager hid himself behind me, shouting last-minute directions from under my right armpit.

"Lights," someone yelled. The arc lights made the dull day a little brighter. "Speed," shouted the Austrian sound director. "Action," bellowed the director from behind me.

Fred, out of camera range, now released the bear. The bear took a few short steps, sniffed the air, head huge upon his snaky neck. He homed in on the chicken with surprising speed and set off in the lolloping gallop that bears have. He made it right up to the cage, sniffing furiously, sensing the chicken was underneath. He was supposed to scrape it out, but he did not. Oh, no. He ran behind the cage and inside, through the open door. The cameraman had not thought to close it. The camera and cameraman were pushed aside. The chicken pieces were snatched up. Everyone was transfixed. The cameraman was trying to right himself, still clutching the heavy camera, when the bear turned to leave, pushing him sideways again. There it stopped. It lifted one leg, revealing to all that it was a male bear, and proceeded to urinate on the cameraman's neck. Chicken in mouth, it then ran down the slope to the river, straight for the shallow bend where I had asked that reinforcements be placed.

Unfortunately, when the original Indian and the two additional ones saw the bear advancing on them at speed, they turned and ran in three different directions. The bear splashed gaily through the shallows, up the bank and into the dense bush. I could have sworn he was grinning as he went. Meanwhile, the cameraman was in shock. He just lay in the cage shaking. Our production manager had emerged from my rear and stood running his hands over his cheeks in the manner of the late film actor S.Z. (Cuddles) Zackell, saying as he did so, "Vat's this going to cost?!"

"Should have got the vet," I said, feeling a trifle venomous.

We filed away for lunch. The cameraman was carried back on a stretcher by two Indians. Lacking a trained first-aid person, he was washed by the gaffer. Clean clothes were purchased for him from the inlet store. It then took the best part of a bottle of rum to bring him round to a state bordering his normal self. Whether by virtue of bear scare or rum, he was off work for the rest of the day.

During lunch, the production manager and his assistants were on the phone and in conference together. Occasionally, they glanced over a shoulder at me as I attacked my pork chop. On reaching the site after lunch, I found a tall, dark-skinned, dignified man waiting. He was muffled up in heavy boots and tweed overcoat, a parka over that and a woolen balaclava helmet of the type favoured by Scott of the Arctic.

He asked for me. I acknowledged him. He extended a slim but powerful hand. "Chief Inspector Hepworth, my dear fellow. I think I am indebted to you for some employment. I am Dr. Rajkumar." He paused. "Veterinarian, University of Zanzibar." I said I was glad to see him and asked what drugs he had brought. We walked over to his Cadillac and he opened the trunk. He had every conceivable drug, device and instrument we were ever likely to need.

From then on, "Doc" and I kept each other company on the set. He suffered a good deal from the cold, but did not complain. Work for veterinarians is not easily come by in the North, where almost any sick animal unlikely to make a quick recovery is shot by its owner. Doc talked of slowly but surely building up his practice. He first had to educate the animal-owning public to care for their pets. He had something of a racial discrimination problem in addition, but he did not complain of that any more than he did the cold.

I advised that the cougar be given a sedative when he was brought out to be filmed with the caged dog. Fred objected, claiming it "would take the edge off keenness." As a consequence, action on the set produced a spitting, snarling fury of a big cat, frustrated at the prospect of being deprived of a meal, which in this case was tenderloin of German shepherd.

This dog, at my insistence, was removed from the set. The cougar quieted somewhat when we surrounded him with snowfencing, only to flare up again when the continuity girl placed her stool near his fence and began to read her script and notes. He slashed out at her, broke the fence, and removed the right sleeve from her nice ski jacket. Fortunately, that was all he removed. She jumped back, white-faced and trembling.

"Why would he do that?" she wondered shakily.

"He's that age, I'm afraid." I had tried to explain that earlier, to deaf ears. The cougar was held by Fred and myself while Doc administered enough sedative to prevent a recurrence of ferocity towards humans. As an additional ounce of prevention, I had all women on the site moved thirty yards away, downwind of the cat. Not that they needed any urging to keep away.

The next day a red fox was to be photographed. An enclosure of wire mesh was erected to contain the fox within the working area. The actual photography went smoothly enough, but when it was time for the handsome beast to be returned to his cage, that was another matter. First Fred alone tried to catch him, then Fred's helper assisted. The two Indians holding the fence up joined in, then an assistant manager, then myself, followed by Doc. At times the action reminded me of a wild Highland eight-some reel, as we wheeled and ducked under each other. We were a sweating, wheezing octet when we finally stuffed Reynard back in his box.

The final day was wolf day. Six wolves had been trained to follow a small electric horn in order to reach their food supply—the inevitable chicken. The group scenes were enchanting to watch. I happen to like wolves, so for me the day was a treat. A later scene called for one large wolf to run down a small track between trees, with the camera tracking backwards, recording his coming. A small railroad line was laid to accommodate the camera and the cameraman, by now recovered. We all stood well back where the vehicles were parked nose-to-tail alongside the widened bushroad. Once again, cries of "lights," "speed," "action" sounded. We waited in expectation to see the magnificent king wolf come bounding out of the trees. He came all right. The trouble was, he just kept coming.

Someone yelled, "Look out," and the next thing I knew Doc was standing on my fingers, on the tree branch I was hanging from.

I managed to look around once I had a more secure hold. I was just in time to see one of the larger, fatter Indians pulling himself by his fingernails up the sheer sides of a property van as the king wolf ran beneath him totally unconcerned. He returned when the food horn sounded.

The next day was "wrap day," as they say in the business. Everyone was busy packing up equipment and property. As for Doc and me, we were busy trying to arrange for the live trapping of our runaway bear, who had been occupied overturning garbage cans and mooching handouts from passing motorists. Natural Resources managed it painlessly. They also placed the animal, by helicopter no less, in a forest reserve well away from hunters, near a stream where fish were spawning.

I bade Doc farewell, after a visit to his fine new clinic and hospital, and flew home. The next day, after putting out the usual fires that spring up when one's away, I set about making out the bill to the film company. A letter to the effect that no inhumane treatment had been used in order to make the animals perform went with it. The total bill, including air fare, motor vehicle and hotel, amounted to a hefty $1,500. The thought struck me that perhaps I should pay them for the fun I'd enjoyed in the last few days. I wondered if I could interest a travel agency in running guided tours of animal films in the making.

Three years later, I was affluent enough to pay a visit to Los Angeles and Universal Studios. While there, I was tempted by the many brochures set before me advertising side trips. One of them was for *Animal Actors:* "See animals in the actual making of films." The publicity handout indicated the tour was a creation of the president of Universal, a multi-billion-dollar company. I thought back to my idea of three years before and the days at Muffin Inlet. There's no doubt about it. Great minds think alike.

A SINGED
NIGHTINGALE

IN THE SUMMER OF 1977 A BUSH FIRE BROKE OUT NEAR the Manitoba border. It hardly attracted a ripple of notice until it started to grow. After three days of burning out of control, it began burning in two directions, west and east. The easterly arm, fanned by the west wind, burned harder and faster. Even so, apart from the Ministry of Natural Resources, forestry engineers and bush pilots, no one paid much attention. No one, that is, except the inhabitants of the tiny community of Batley.

Batley was a small logging and sawmill town seventy-five miles from any other community on the map. It was fifteen miles from a paved road. It had a post office that operated out of a lean-to, a travelling store that called twice a week, and a mobile library that came once a week. No centre for cultural affairs, no cinema, no pub, just twenty-eight houses, a sawmill, a workshop, and piles and piles of cut and rough lumber. In a place like Batley one is bound to be concerned with the elements. After all, they govern the livelihood of the place. So when the Forestry Service reported the fire some thirty miles west of their community, the residents were interested enough to take a look at it—after supper.

When it had burned more or less out of control for three days, some of the more athletic members of the settlement were motivated to climb the one-hundred-and-forty-foot fire tower to look through the long-range binoculars at the line of flames slowly advancing towards them.

Two days later the fire had advanced to within seven miles of the settlement. One or two of the older folks who lived with their children decided it was time to visit cousin Mable in Mississauga. The corporal in charge of the OPP detachment circulated a message to all residents. It was to the effect that they should be prepared to evacuate their homes on short notice. Any pets, it noted, must be left behind.

All day long, from sun-up, the water bombers swooped down on Baltic Lake, filled up with water, flew over and dropped the several tons on the line of flames still creeping east. The water bombers and seventy firefighters slowed the advance, but they were powerless to stop it. Residents hoped it would rain. It did not.

Gunnar Neilson tended his vegetable garden at the rear of his neat wooden house. A stolid Dane, he routinely worked in his garden every evening after supper, keeping himself and two friends in root and green vegetables for most of the year. Neilson worked on rhythmically hoeing the soil between the rows of giant cabbages. Pipe in mouth, head down, he did not notice the pack of timber wolves running over his plot until the third almost collided with him. He called to his wife, who was watering flowers, as several more of the handsome beasts loped by. "Must be getting close when the wolves run into town," he observed. His wife agreed and, being of a practical nature, went indoors and packed them two emergency bags. She topped up the seed and water containers for her budgies and hoped the evacuation would not be necessary.

At three a.m. the mill siren sounded. The evacuation signal soon came from the OPP loudspeaker car. It was time to go. But not by car—the fire had jumped the dirt road, the only way out. Falling and burning trees blocked the road as predicted. Everyone was to go to the baseball diamond. A Canadian Forces helicopter would take everyone out. But again, no pets. The animals would have to remain. Pet owners were distraught. Surely they could take a small dog or a cat in a basket. No, the OPP repeated, animals were not to be transported.

It was at this turn of events that Charley Crawley made it known that, if his two goats and Shetland pony couldn't go along on the chopper, well, he wouldn't go either. Charley earned a precarious living as a jack of all trades. Basically, he enjoyed the solitude of the bush but detested work in the sawmill. He sold the milk from two goats, which he delivered in a small cart pulled by the pony. He did painting, gardening, ditch-cleaning and street-sweeping, what there was of it. No one really knew how old he was. He had looked sixty as long as anyone could remember.

Charley watched as the disquieted residents drove or walked to the ball field. It dawned on him that none of the dog owners had their dogs with them. He ran forward. "Where's your dog, there?" he asked. Owners replied, "Chained to his doghouse," "In the porch," "In the driveway." It saddened them to have to leave their animals in this fashion.

"Don't worry," reassured Charley. "I'm not going. I'll see he's all right. Where's his food?" Most residents fed their animals table scraps, so they had little in the way of commercial pet food, but undaunted Charley circulated amongst the assembly until he had a list of every animal left behind. The Neilsons gave him a key to their house, in order that the budgies could be visited for feeding. Others did the same, providing letters of authority hastily scrawled on the backs of bills, envelopes or anything at hand.

The big Chinook helicopter could be heard long before it could be seen in the night sky. With its two large landing lights switched on, it resembled a large flying beetle about to pounce on an aphid. The evacuees, clutching bundles and suitcases, crouched low on the edge of the ball field. Charley Crawley stole silently away, hiding himself between two piles of cut timber.

It took three trips to evacuate the entire community. The last to leave were the OPP corporal and his two constables. They circulated through the buildings, calling to Charley through bullhorns, pleading with him to join them. Charley pushed his small terrier under his jacket and huddled lower in his hiding hole. He did not emerge until the sounds of the helicopter had faded away completely.

Next day, after a meagre breakfast of goat's milk porridge and tea, Charley toured the houses, filling up water bowls, talking to the chained dogs and pouring a little goat's milk for the cats that remained.

The weather continued hot and bright. There was now the ever-present smell of smoke. Ash blew in the wind. Plainly, the fire was close.

Taking stock of the situation, Charley decided to assemble all the animals in a clear space so as to afford them a reasonable chance of survival when the fire burst through the underbrush. Using his pony and cart, Charley worked all day to move dogs and doghouses onto the baseball field. Where a dog had no kennel, Charley improvised—old machine crates, empty steel drums. An old Volkswagon car, rusted and unused, became home for three huskies. Charley watered every animal three times a day, and fed them once a day. On the fourth day his dog food was almost used up. That was when he heard the phone ring.

He was in the Neilsons' house tending the budgies. After some initial hesitation, he picked up the phone. "Hello, who's calling?" he asked. It was a journalist from Winnipeg telephoning on behalf of his newspaper. How was Charley and his little group of abandoned animals, the reporter wanted to know. "We're fine," said Charley. "How did you know I'm here?" The evacuees, safely housed in a Canadian Forces base, had spoken of him, with concern for their animals. Some clever calculations by the reporter had effected communications. "Do you need anything?" asked his interviewer. "Sure," replied Charley, "dog and cat food." The reporter agreed he would try to arrange a supply. He was careful not to say how.

That evening, Canadian television stations announced the plight of Charley and his little group. Humane Societies everywhere were bombarded with telephone calls from people demanding to know what was to be done for the dogs and cats of Batley.

I missed a good deal of this because Stu and I were in south-central Ontario posing as farmers at livestock auctions where we had information cockfights would be held. We had followed a group of "cockers" from auction to auction in anticipation of fights being held in the sales ring at close of business. But each day brought difficulties to prevent the fights, and what had been anticipated as a short operation was now lengthened. Our director had flown off to one of his meetings and was unavailable for comment. The brunt of the phone calls fell on the new boy, Swoop Nightingale.

Robert François Nightingale hailed from a small farm near Coaticook, Quebec. He had applied for an appointment with the Society, and having a B.A. in Zoology had been accepted on probation in an acting capacity. Being a junior, he was in no position to respond to the press; he could only record the messages. Unfortunately, he had no one to pass them to. After two days he was frustrated to the point of action at any price. With a small bag packed, he arrived at the office early, left a message and went to the airport. Using a credit card, he got himself on a plane to Kookunant.

Our local shelter manager in Kookunant had a small stock of kibble and tinned food, not enough to feed the Batley animals. Undeterred, Swoop promptly purchased several large bags of dog food, a case of tinned cat food and a can opener. Later, he told me he didn't really know just what he would do with his pile of supplies, just that he felt he had to assemble them. He begged several empty grain sacks from a feed mill to reinforce the heavy paper kibble bags.

While on his way back to the shelter from the feed mill, his eye fell on an advertisement for pleasure flights by a private pilot. Fifteen dollars, the ad read. Swoop wasted no time. The pilot, however, was not keen. For one thing, it was twice the distance of his normal air tour. Swoop agreed to pay twice the price. It was an offence to drop things down from aircraft without a permit. "You're not doing the dropping," countered Swoop, "I am." Still the pilot demurred. Finally, Swoop agreed to pay any legal costs and fines that might result. Only when Swoop had agreed to this in writing did the pilot invite Swoop to place his limited supply of pet food in the cabin.

The small twin-engine Piper Comanche roared west. Batley was in sight after forty minutes flying time. They circled the community, flying low, noticing the kennels and barking occupants, most standing outside their houses. Charley could be seen standing in the centre, shading his eyes, looking up at the small plane.

Swoop had hoped to drop the packages on the turf of the field, so as to cushion the shock of the fall somewhat. However, the assembly of kennels precluded this. It was decided a dusty strip of dirt road to the north of the field would perhaps be best.

Swoop had a stout rope lashed around his waist. The other end of the rope had been securely tied around the base of the pilot's seat. This permitted Swoop to step within a foot of the doorway. The pilot throttled back for the run in. Swoop hesitantly stood up and pushed the three sacks containing dog food and one case of cat food into position on the floor just inside the door.

The approach was at treetop height. "Open the door now," shouted the pilot. Swoop slid the cargo door to the open position. A rush of hot air and noise filled the small cabin. "Get ready," shouted the pilot at the top of his lungs. Swoop could almost hear him. Swoop sat down, arms braced out behind him, feet against the first sack, knees bent. "Away," roared the pilot. Swoop straightened his legs. The sacks stacked one behind the other were pushed quickly through the open door. All were sucked into the slipstream momentarily and fluttered to the dirt road. Charley could be seen waving his hands as they turned for home.

The fire did not go out, nor did it go away. It slowed its approach as the winds died down temporarily.

It was about this time that I was able to phone the office and check in. May, our receptionist, told me the situation. The director had made no contact. I asked May to take my confidential folder out of the vault and open an envelope marked "National Defence." She read me the names of all the various liaison officers in National Defence Headquarters and their duties. Finally, she reached "mercy flights, Captain Raymond Patenaude." She gave me the phone number. I telephoned Defence Headquarters in Ottawa and asked to speak to Captain Patenaude. He was not in. The sergeant answering for the captain was most understanding, grasping the essentials of my request. Unfortunately, he could not approve such a mission, but his superior would be informed the minute he returned. "In the interim, we must be patient."

Stu met me on return to the Community Sales Barn. Having been watching beef calves for auction, Stu not only looked like a beef farmer, he smelled like one. I motioned him into the coffee shop. We ordered ham and eggs, with lots of coffee, and I outlined the situation for him. Some city tourists entered and sat down at the table next to us. One middle-aged lady wrinkled her nose. "The food drains are blocked or something." Stu and I looked at each other as we devoured our late breakfast. As we rose to pay our bill, I heard the woman say, "The air is clearer now. Must have been those two farm men. Not the drains at all." Her husband looked happier as he chewed his omelet.

Back at head office we experienced more of the same. Windows were opened, deodorant bottles were brought out. We isolated ourselves in my office. No reply from Ottawa. Another long-distance call. Captain Patenaude had still not returned. We set off for our respective homes to bathe and change. My wife, seeing me approaching, threw my track suit and jogging shoes outside. "If you smell as bad as you look," she said, "you had best change out in the tack room." My dirty clothes went into a closed garbage bag. Since the stable cat would not enter the tack room while my boots remained there, I was obliged to air the boots outside on the roof. Only then was I allowed indoors.

Washed, shaved, bathed and changed, I returned to the office. The director called. I briefed him on the situation.

"Who authorized Swoop's trip to Kookunant," he demanded to know.

"No one," I answered.

"Bloody hell," he roared. "How much will that cost?"

I said I hadn't the bills yet.

"Well, find out," he ordered.

As he rang off, I heard the operator say that the cost of the call would be eighteen dollars—from Denver, Colorado.

Back in Kookunant, Swoop had been discovered by the media correspondents, who wanted to know when he would make another supply drop. They wanted to go along. He called me on the phone, anxious to know if he was doing the right thing. Listening to his story, I decided that one photojournalist wouldn't be a bad thing, but one only. The aircraft wasn't big enough for the eight or so assembled to cover the story. It also occurred to me that perhaps the goats and the pony might need hay. Five bales of hay would fill up the plane and preclude any other passengers.

Once again, Swoop lashed himself to the plane's interior; the photographer was pursuaded to do likewise. Swoop, feet braced in position, was photographed on the run in, the actual drop in progress, and from several very dramatic angles as the plane lurched in the thermal air currents. Swoop was actually balanced on his buttocks at one point, on the door sill, on the rope's extreme. Due to the camera angle, the rope was not visible. Swoop appeared to be the daring young man in the flying machine indeed.

The director telephoned again the next day. I reported my lack of progress. I asked if he had any suggestions for speeding up the Defence Department. "Leave it to me," he grunted, "I'll talk to old— —he owes me a favour!" (He mentioned a well-known political figure.) Swoop telephoned, very worried by now, as the pilot had jacked up his rates to three times the original price.

Next day, Captain Patenaude had still not returned, but Swoop was on the front page of the Toronto daily papers. In a fit of inspiration, I telephoned Winnipeg, the Department of National Defence base nearest Kookunant. "Oh, you need Captain Patenaude," said the military operator when I called. "I'll connect you to his number." "Patenaude here," said an unmistakably Quebecois voice. I outlined my problem. The rescue was set for eight o'clock the following morning. I told Swoop to be ready with all necessary carrying cages, sky kennels, tethering ropes, sacks and suitable accommodation for the rescued animals.

The late-night television news brought ominous warnings. The winds would increase to gusts in excess of sixty kilometres an hour. The flames would be fanned.

The next morning found me sitting by the phone in my office. It was cool there, but I had a nervous sweat. At nine-fifteen Swoop called. The helicopter had been delayed due to engine problems. Takeoff had been rescheduled to eleven a.m. I tried to concentrate on the morning mail. Eleven-twenty, Swoop called again. Aircraft still not serviceable. A part was being flown by jet from Cold Lake, Alberta. My nails were showing signs of definite wear. The director called. I briefed him, adding that no one from Ottawa or Parliament Hill had been in touch. Since the aircraft's arrival was imminent, however, any action in Ottawa would appear redundant. He didn't agree and rang off in a bad humour.

May had a radio at her desk. I went to hear the noonday

news. It was grim. The fire had worsened, fanned by the increasing westerly winds, and was due to peak about four p.m.

Back in Batley, old Charley went about his chores, watering the livestock, feeding the hay to his goats and the pony. He had brought the Neilsons' birds down to the little camp he had made on the baseball diamond, and he talked to his charges as he went about his tasks; but Charley knew the wind force was increasing. The air was filled with smoke and flying ash. No doubt about it, the fire was getting close. But he wasn't worried. After all, on the diamond they were clear of the trees.

Out on the Trans-Canada Highway, the OPP were very worried. They had blocked off the road. Visibility in the fire's vicinity was nil. Besides, with the increase in wind strength a small vehicle might be sucked into the firestorm and incinerated.

For me, the afternoon was a slow, nerve-racking one. At three-fifteen, the phone rang. It was Swoop. The helicopter was in sight and he was prepared to leave. I looked at my watch. Forty minutes flying time would put the rescue attempt over Batley at the peak wind time.

Swoop was assisted in transporting his cages and kennels by the five crewmen aboard the Chinook. He was shown to a seat near the pilot's compartment and at long last the rescue mission was in motion. The site was easy to see. One simply flew at the wall of smoke on the horizon and worked crosswind from there.

Charley was sitting out front of his little camp in an old deck chair he had resurrected from who knows where, smoking his pipe and dozing in the smoking heat. He stared up at the loud roar. He turned. The Neilsons' house was in flames, yet the fire was not visible in the fringe of bush. As he looked, a second house burst into flames. Suddenly, Charley understood. Naked flames weren't necessary; intense heat was the danger. The dogs whined and barked, the cats huddled. Charley ran out the garden hose he'd borrowed and began to spray every animal and his camp with a fine spray. Then the water ran out.

Swoop and helicopter crew sighted Charley about the same time. The big machine descended, blades swishing and whirring, causing the goats to run off and the pony to prance and rear at the end of his tethering rope.

Landing as far down the diamond as possible, the Chinook settled on the dusty turf. Swoop and the crewmen alighted immediately, hunched forward against the smoke-filled wind. Animals were hastily placed in cages, boxes and bags. Charley was almost unaware as he ran after his goats, who trotted through the gardens of remaining houses, bleating miserably. Finally, all that remained were the goats and the pony. Two crewmen each lifted a goat tied in a large sack with its head protruding. The pony was a different problem. He was too heavy to lift and objected to the whole process by kicking and rearing. Eventually, two rope slings were affixed round his barrel-like mid-section and the crane winch lifted him up to be swung aboard by the crewmen.

It seemed all had been safely gathered in when old Charley remembered the Neilsons' birds. Swoop took off at a flat-out run for the camp. Old Charley was helped aboard, protesting that he couldn't leave without the little birds. The pilot nervously eyed the wooden mill buildings, which seemed next in line to burst into flames, whereupon the tongues of fire from a larger building might just reach farther across the field and endanger the chopper. "Let's be getting out of here," said the pilot. "Wait, sir," called the senior crewman. "The inspector has gone to get some birds." The pilot cursed to himself but stayed his hand on the throttle.

Two cow moose, with leggy, nervous, trotting calves beside them, thundered past the front of the aircraft. The bull, hornless in the summer but still formidable, galloped behind the small group. Rabbits, mice and squirrels could also be seen rushing west to east.

The mill shot up in flames with a crack like a field gun.

"That does it," said the pilot. "We're in danger. Drop the winch." The big machine whirred skywards as the winch payed out its recovery hook and harness down into the spot vacated.

They had reached a hundred and fifty feet, or thereabouts, when Swoop returned with the budgie cage. He was sweating and breathless, his hair full of ash, his face black with smoke and dust. For a couple of seconds he looked dumbly at the dangling harness, then he strapped himself in. Clutching the flimsy budgie cage, he was hoisted aloft and swung aboard the flying pet farm to safety and congratulations from the crew. Meanwhile, his original pilot and a full complement of newsmen had witnessed the rescue. They had photographed the whole process. That evening, all the news programs showed Swoop Nightingale, in glorious, living colour, dangling from the helicopter on a slim thread of steel cable, firmly clutching the two little budgies in their small cage. Next day, the office phones rang and rang with congratulations. A week later, the donations began arriving from all parts of North America.

The director and Swoop both arrived back at head office almost simultaneously. The director was a few moments ahead. "Where's that bloody Nightingale?" were his first angry words. Plainly, he hadn't seen either the television or the morning papers, having arrived on an overnight plane from the western United States, where presumably he'd been too engaged in important matters to watch television.

"He's due here any time," I answered, "so are the press. They want to meet him."

"They can have him when I'm finished with him," interjected the director. "I'll approve press conferences around here."

I pushed a selection of daily papers across his desk. Each one depicted Swoop in some exciting pose or another —dirty, dusty, scared but triumphant. The headlines ran from "For the Birds" to "A Singed Nightingale." Amid much harrumphing and "I see," the director calmed down. He greeted Swoop warmly, and the press with his cordial smile and genial wit. We all stood around, the supporting cast, smiling our polite smiles.

Three days later the accrued bills for the Kookunant operation arrived on the director's desk. The paying of them all was a less romantic story indeed.

A JAGUAR
FOR
CHRISTMAS

IT WAS A BITTER DAY WITH A HINT OF SNOW IN THE offing. I was looking through the kitchen window before breakfast when the phone rang. It was the OPP in Elm Valley.

"Good morning, sir. How are you this morning?"

I groaned a little. From experience I know that when the police greet you that way they need you.

"You tell me what the problem is," I replied, "and I'll tell you how I am."

"Well, sir," he went on, "we have an escaped jaguar."

"I'm not very well," I said.

Nevertheless, after hearing his story I agreed to be at his detachment office at ten a.m. He agreed to provide additional men to beat the bushes if they should require beating.

I phoned my assistant, Stu. The only trouble with Stu is that he's slightly mad. Anything that's exotic and smells of circus he immediately adopts and wants to make his own. He loses interest for the time being in anything else, including his wife. Stu was delighted with the idea of a day given over to jaguar hunting.

I chewed my breakfast absent-mindedly, oblivious of the tasty mushrooms and bacon my wife had prepared. She was miffed by my failure to appreciate her cooking, but, as I pointed out to her, she didn't have to conduct a jaguar hunt in a suburban estate on a very wintry New Year's Eve.

Stu arrived at nine. I took the trusty Palmer-Capchur gun from the cupboard and placed it, with the tranquillizer darts, in my faithful station wagon. "What time will you be back?" asked my wife. "Remember, we're due at the McLintocks' for drinks at seven and dinner at eight. We mustn't be late." I mumbled something about being back as fast as I could and went out to welcome Stu, who was grinning like a steel trap and fairly bubbling over with excitement.

We made good time to the Elm Valley OPP detachment. It was situated on the edge of the pretty little village. Only the biting wind from adjoining Lake Huron spoiled the idyllic effect of the scene.

Inside the station the senior of the two duty constables gave us more details about the escape of the jaguar. Close by, on the lake edge, was a new subdivision situated in pine woods. The homes were winterized but mainly intended as summer, vacation, or retirement homes. One of these had been bought by a family from London who now were waiting to be safely escorted out of their house—and saved from a jaguar. They were just finishing their packing up when we arrived with one of the OPP officers. Their holiday was in ruins.

The father told us that the previous evening had been normal, with the kids in bed yawning over their books—for there was no TV here, just the wind in the pines. About ten o'clock their small terrier, who had been snoozing by the fire, had commenced a furious barking and scratching at the door. Finally, unable to stand the racket any longer, and a little worried, the father had opened the door to have a look outside. In dashed a jaguar. Out went the terrified terrier.

Where the little dog had gone no one knew, for the father had forbidden any of the family to go looking. The jaguar had rushed past the stunned parents, up the stairs and into the youngest child's bedroom. The mother had run upstairs after the animal, screaming and shouting. Before following her, Father had stopped to snatch up used supper dishes from the dining table. Dishes in one arm, he had used the other to pelt the intruding cat with the crockery. He had just about gone through the entire dinner service when his assault succeeded and the jaguar loped out of the boy's bedroom.

By this time Mother had joined the battle herself. Taking her cue from Father, she had thrown bottles of ginger ale, Coke and beer at the jaguar, and it had finally left the house the same way it had arrived. After that the family had barricaded one door with a piano, the other with a chesterfield. Then they had just sat and shivered, wide awake, for the rest of a very long night. At the end of it one immediate blessing was awarded them. At first light their little dog was found shaking on the doorstep, none the worse for his encounter with the jaguar.

There was but one phone in this new subdivision and that was in a phone booth a quarter of a mile away. At dawn, with no cat in sight, the father had slipped into his car and driven, windows up, to the phone booth. There he had telephoned the police and they, after consulting their procedure manual, had called me.

We already knew something of the jaguar. It had escaped once before, the preceding summer. On that occasion it had found a semi-blind spaniel in a neighbour's garden and had played with it until the spaniel died mercifully of a heart attack. Orders under the O.S.P.C.A. Act had followed to ensure that the beautiful spotted feline was retained in an adequate cage, and until now the poodles, terriers and other pets in the vicinity had remained safe.

We reassured the family as much as we could, and Stu and I drove to the jaguar owner's house. His German shepherd was chained to an outdoor doghouse, but the owner wasn't home.

We gingerly scouted around and found that a roof panel from the outdoor jaguar cage was missing, and that a basement window that provided entrance to and exit from the cage adjoining the house was open. We went back to town to obtain a search warrant, and on returning we were joined by no less than twenty officers, brought in from the nearby district headquarters. A helicopter rumbled overhead.

I asked for a "sound" vehicle with a broadcast system mounted on it. A van soon drove up. We met and conferred with the corporal now in charge and requested that the van be driven around the town continuously advising house-owners to keep children, cats and dogs indoors. We crossed the sidewalk back to the jaguar's house and donned our coveralls.

Two semi-retired residents, four policemen, a reporter and a stray phone repairman watched Stu and me stroll in what we hoped was a nonchalant manner towards the open basement window, where we believed the jaguar had entered the house after his nocturnal adventure. I was carrying my stained and battered stock cane, which I contrived to twirl between my fingers as we marched forward. I attempted to whistle "The Man Who Broke the Bank at Monte Carlo." Stu lugged the Palmer and trooped behind.

Sliding through the basement window, I was filled with uneasiness. Once inside, though it wasn't a well-lighted area, I could make out bones, feathers, then an empty pail, and further, a broken chain. All evidence of a hungry animal gone foraging. While I was concentrating on every detail of the basement scene, my back was turned to the window. Stu quietly squeezed through and fell on me. I was glad it was Stu.

We went up the basement steps and found the door to the first floor locked. The jaguar had discovered the same thing and, by chewing and clawing on the double-skin plywood, had managed to remove the bottom two feet of the door. I somehow wriggled under the broken section and opened it from the other side.

A tap was running. The big cat at least had water. She had also amused herself by relocating the washer and dryer. The kitchen garbage had been well examined. Potato peelings, tea leaves and paper diapers were scattered around, and there were jaguar droppings throughout the living room and bedrooms. The dented and twisted air conditioner, lying in the kitchen sink, showed the method of exit used by the South American feline.

We opened the front door and informed the waiting police that the house was empty. They came up to the open doorway, sniffed the aroma of garbage and jaguar, and promptly left. We closed the open window and locked the door behind us, then we too left the empty premises.

Our short conference in the street was reduced to lip-reading until the helicopter moved further up the Lake Huron beach. Using a map of the subdivision, we arranged for pairs of policemen to walk through the newly built sections while Stu and I, with the police corporal, began checking the older properties that had both established gardens and crawl spaces.

For Stu and me the search involved a routine walk round each house, checking the powder-soft snow for tracks of any kind. Even dog tracks were followed. And tracks of any sort meant a check of the space beneath the nearest house. As I would lie flat on my stomach, patrolling footsteps would be heard and a glance upward would usually reveal a highly polished pair of boots, navy blue trousers with red stripes down their seams, and the muzzle of a gun pointing straight down. I cringed every time a policeman's steps came near. By the end of the morning I felt as if I had lost a good deal of weight. My stomach was once more a nodding acquaintance of my spine, and I could now distinguish the difference between a Remington and a Mosberg solely by their sights.

By one o'clock the helicopter pilot had left, evidently having decided he wasn't making any significant contribution to the event. A policeman arrived with box lunches. The cold, keen wind had given me an appetite, and I wolfed my meal along with the others. As I drank my coffee and racked my brain for a solution to our jaguar problem, a television reporter and a cameraman descended on me. The reporter was fashionably dressed in a trench coat with an enormous fur collar.

"Tell me, Inspector," the reporter rumbled, "do you think this dangerous cat is still here, or could it simply have swum away across Georgian Bay? After all, these jaguars are good swimmers, aren't they?" He held out his hand microphone to catch the words of wisdom he hoped would fall from my lips.

"Yes," I said, a bit uncertainly, "these felines are good swimmers, but we think the jaguar is still here."

"What makes you so certain, Inspector?"

I wasn't so certain, and didn't think I had sounded so, but the public needed protection not reassurance. He was doing the hard-nosed, questioning reporter bit, keeping on at me.

"Well," I said, "you see, there are no tracks on the beach or snow leading into the water."

"Oh, I see. And where are the tracks?" he asked.

"Nowhere, actually. We haven't seen any tracks we are sure of. That's why we think the animal is still here."

"Tell me, Inspector, is this cat dangerous?" He was now after titillating news for the evening report.

"Certainly," I said.

"Will it attack?" He was enjoying himself now.

"Of course, under certain circumstances," I said wearily.

"And what is likely to provoke an attack?"

"Fur coat-collars," I said, unable to stop myself.

The hard-nosed newsman switched off his tape recorder and hastily climbed back into his multicoloured car. The cameraman was left to fend for himself.

The twenty policemen were becoming bored with the situation. They were now standing guard at intersections in hopes of seeing the jaguar cross from one lot to another. Privately, I thought it would be dusk before the animal made a move, if then. Questioning the neighbours had revealed that the jaguar owners had departed for Hull, Quebec, on Christmas Eve morning. They had told the neighbours that they had left ten days' supply of meat and a whole pail of water for "Evita," their jaguar.

The owners, though apparently well-meaning, plainly knew little of the ways of wild carnivores. Left this way, any such wild animal will simply gorge itself on all the meat available, digest it and then be hungry again when the food has passed through its system—approximately forty-eight hours later, depending upon the animal's activity.

As we stood there steadily getting colder, I was struck with an idea nothing short of pure genius. At least *I* thought so, the others weren't enthusiastic. "Since the German shepherd wasn't attacked by the jaguar when it went through the window," I said, "they must be friends. Suppose we let the dog go? It might lead us to the cat."

At least Stu was willing and the others reluctantly agreed. Stu fished a length of binder twine from the pocket of his parka. Releasing the dog from his chain, Stu tied one end of the twine to the dog's collar and walked him to the door of the house visited by the jaguar the previous evening. The dog turned sharply northwest from there and ran, towing Stu behind him.

He stopped after a run of two hundred yards, looking at a crawl space, one we had not noticed, under a new, unoccupied cottage. I lay down on my stomach for the umpteenth time and peered into the dark. A rasping hiss rewarded me, and when my eyes became accustomed to the reduced light, I made out one green eye and the triangle of a pricked-up feline ear.

Stu tied the dog to a fence and lay down alongside me. "See her?" I asked. "There, behind that concrete block support."

"Oh, yes!" exclaimed Stu. He was happy at last. We conferred as we lay there, half under the cottage, our unprotected heads within fifteen feet of some very large, white fangs.

Leaving Stu to keep watch on the animal, I slid out and went to speak to the police corporal. "She's under there all right. Can you get your men to surround this property quietly? And warn the occupants in the vicinity to stay indoors, no matter what!" This was done with surprising speed and efficiency, thanks largely to the walkie-talkies carried by the police.

Next, I set about borrowing planks and boxes from neighbouring buildings, until finally I had blocked in all the crawl space immediately under the cottage, with the exception of some space around Stu and a very small space to the left of the big cat.

I took out the "vet's lasso" from my car and re-coiled it. A vet's lasso differs from the rough "cowboy" type in that the sliding ring running down the main rope is actually two pieces of metal locked by a small spring lever. When the lever is flipped, the pieces fall apart, quickly releasing the animal caught in the noose. I set it down opposite the hole we had left for the jaguar, then I picked up my stock-cane and rejoined Stu where he lay still on watch.

"She keeps having a look out, then dodging back behind that post," Stu reported as I wriggled alongside him.

"Yes," I replied, "that's what she did with me. I daren't use the tranquillizer gun under here. I might hit her in the eye, and I don't think the Ketomyn will work in her skull, anyway."

"No," Stu agreed, "the idea you described to me seems best, but perhaps we had better put a rope on you in case we have to drag you out."

He squirmed out and passed me the end of an animal rope we had brought with us. I fastened it round my waist and a system of pull signals was hastily improvised with two policemen who were detailed to lay down their guns and hold an end of the rope. Stu said, "We're ready!"

Taking a deep breath and thinking, 'Here goes nothing,' I started my slow wriggle towards the green staring eyes. A deep hiss indicated I was getting too close. I wriggled on. The hiss escalated to snarls, and finally the snarls to spitting roars. I wondered seriously if I was doing the right thing. But who had ever been in this situation before? No one that I know. Was there a right way to pursue a jaguar through a crawl space? I held my stock cane out in front of me with both hands as I slowly wormed along on my elbows and knees. Finally I began to tap the stonework. This caused the jaguar to give ground a little.

"Are you all right?" shouted someone down my entrance hole. "It's getting cold out here."

I didn't shout back for fear of provoking a crawling charge, but merely gave a short pull on the rope that meant O.K. To myself, though, I thought of a good many other replies as the sweat of exertion and fear dripped off the end of my nose. My neck ached with the effort of holding my head back. This had to be one of the great moments in the history of big-game hunting and I wanted to go to the john.

My cane extended past the stone pillar, and the cat backed away. "Back up!" I said, "Git!" and some other words of international use, in an effort to cause a backwards exit. I was soon past the post. Evita and I faced each other in the crawl space. Both green eyes were fixed, unmoving and unblinking, on me. The gleaming white canine teeth appeared to be about four inches long. I was tiring quickly now and beginning to feel a bit desperate. Finally I hit the cat square on the end of her nose with the cane. She sneezed, turned, and with a paddling motion of her hind legs went unerringly to the small exit we had provided.

"Here she comes," I managed to announce. I heard a grunt and then a short swear word, followed by a splitting screech. I knew Stu had roped her, and only roughly. We were not done. I wriggled backwards to my entrance and emerged. I wanted to stop and stretch, but there was no time.

I quickly uncoiled my life line and fashioned another noose. After three attempts I managed to snare her gyrating head and move the noose in such a way that it encircled one shoulder, which would prevent strangulation. Then I did the same with Stu's rope. Both these last two manoeuvres were accomplished with aid of my ever-useful stock cane.

We tied one rope to a fence, the other to a tree. I made ready the injection of Ketomyn and Atrovet. Stu, wearing heavy gauntlet gloves, grasped Evita by the roots of her tail and I pushed home the syringe. Six long minutes later, she slumped asleep.

The police had vanished like mist on a warm morning. After a moment of unspoken relief Stu and I heaved Evita into the rear section of his wagon, where she continued to slumber.

Back at the OPP station the corporal finally finished making his notes. I told him we were bound for Cambridge via 400 and 401 highways as fast as possible and would appreciate any help they could provide. Alert to the hazards of transporting a recovered jaguar on Highway 400, the officer advised his district radio operator that the four OPP cars on duty should watch out for us.

We drove as swiftly as possible to Cambridge. En route we made a short stop to boost the Atrovet injection, when Evita showed signs of revival. At six that evening we handed her over to our friend Phillipo, the tigerman, who housed her in a large outdoor cage complete with a heated wooden house and deep straw bedding.

Leaving Evita to recover in hands devoted to big cats, we drove home tired and stiff, but content with a job well done.

"Where have you been?" exclaimed my wife when I walked in. "You're black as a chimney sweep." A tot of scotch and a hot bath did wonders for me.

At seven forty-five we were standing in the McLintocks' living room enjoying aperitifs. Over dinner the menfolk talked of their day's skiing, snowmobiling and butterfly mounting. "What did *you* do today?" one of them asked me. "Rode your horse, I suppose."

I smiled and took a long sip at the excellent sherry. "Something like that," I agreed.

THE SEAWAY ZOO

THE SEAWAY ZOOLOGICAL PARK AND GARDENS comprised about a hundred acres, more or less, of scrub bush, rock outcrop, beaver ponds and small clearings. It wasn't really much of anything. It was owned and operated by an alcoholic Dutchman named John.

John had always wanted wild animals of his own. He was really a furniture maker, but in time he acquired first a Japanese crab-eating monkey, then a llama, and then a camel. After that came a lion, which gave birth to five cubs. A pair of North American buffalo followed, and then a young female grizzly bear. Before he knew it he had a zoo. As he continued to drink, his addiction to rye whisky going from bad to worse, his furniture-making business declined. The animals, however, were not so exacting in their demands as his furniture clients, so John sold his furniture business and concentrated wholeheartedly on the zoo.

He traded off all his male lion cubs for an adult male, a handsome fellow with a tinge of black in his tawny mane. Then he built a battery of monkey cages. A pair of young Hymadradas baboons joined the lone crab-eater monkey, and a foul-smelling male mandrill, with an even fouler temper, occupied another cage.

By the time the events in this tale took place, John's zoo was fairly well known in the locality. He had borrowed forty thousand dollars from the local bank and had set about constructing a tropical house. He was motivated at the time by the offer of a female hippopotamus, said to be in calf, from a zoo in Quebec. Her price was a mere three thousand dollars.

Working sixteen hours a day, John had the tropical house and other housing ready by the opening of the summer season. By a stroke of chance, a member of Parliament who was not enjoying a very high profile at that moment volunteered to open the park. He arranged for coverage by the media to be laid on as well.

On the appointed day, the main gate, decked out with bunting and flags of all nations, welcomed the Honourable Member. A military band from the district was engaged to play at the proceedings. For this event they had decided on contemporary music, but sadly, because of poor arrangements for brass and limited practice time, they were restricted to only three pieces: "Home in Pasadena," "Do You Know the Way to San Jose," and "Wonderful, Wonderful Copenhagen."

The Honourable Member was a little late, and by the time the band had run through this uninspired medley five times, the crowd was getting restless. John, who had been on tenterhooks all morning and had partaken of a little cool beverage to calm his nerves, had since partaken of a little more. He was by now thoroughly drunk and becoming belligerent with it.

"Where is your politician, then?" he demanded of the party faithful, who were present in large numbers and canvassing the crowd. "He'll be here," they reassured him nervously, hoping for the best. Some of them, privy to party secrets, knew that the Honourable Member also calmed his nerves liquidly, often to excess.

At last the Honourable Member arrived in a chauffeur-driven car. John was by this time running up and down along the drive with the llama in an effort to bolster the interest of the crowd, who were becoming thoroughly bored. The elderly male llama resented being thus exercised in the hot sun and began to show his displeasure by bucking and roaring. As the Honourable Member arrived, the llama's complaints were reaching an earsplitting pitch.

The well-oiled parliamentarian, seeing an opportunity with the media, leapt from his car. He posed himself for the cameras, using the llama as backdrop and shaking hands with John, who was in a similar condition. The overheated llama dribbled green slimy spit all down the Honourable Member's nice light-grey flannel suit. Upon noticing this, the politician left, declaring the park open in twenty words. It really seems as though this bad start was an omen for the park.

The hippopotamus escaped not long afterward. It blocked Highway 2 and the OPP had to be called to clear the traffic. What could have resulted in tragedy on the road resulted instead in publicity that was a blessing for the zoo. Media coverage showed the traffic-halting hippo in some detail, and the following week-end customers arrived from all over Ontario and upper New York State.

Two weeks later, John, under the influence of half a bottle, let the buffalo loose. A car transport from Oakville, bound for Montreal, hit the bull square on. That night John fed what was left of him to the lions. By some miracle of providence no humans were hurt.

Throughout all this, John's family, his wife, son and two daughters, helped in every way. But they grew tired of his constant fault-finding, his drunkenness and his unrelenting meanness.

One evening, after a stormy session at the supper table, John stamped out of the house in a temper, slipped on the staircase and fell down a flight of seven steps to the rock outcrop the house was built on. He fell heavily, striking the right side of his head, and the resulting concussion put him in the hospital for three days. All the while he was gone, his family cared for the animals in the park. That is to say, they fed and watered them. Some they cleaned and some they left, especially the dangerous and aggressive animals like the mandrill.

John returned home in an ill humour. He immediately went on a tour of the pens and cages. When he returned to the house, his family, expecting praise for their efforts, were shocked to find themselves accused of idleness and dishonesty. John's family soon returned to their native Holland, and John was alone—but not for long.

He sulked for a week or so, after which he took a good-looking divorcée into his house, partly as housekeeper and bedmate, and partly as ticket-seller and dispenser of pet food at the public entrance.

For a few short weeks all was well. But the rye was still being consumed in quantity and cage hygiene declined in inverse ratio to the fluid consumed. The drinking water was not changed very often, and when it began to exhibit a green scum the public was not amused.

One day, while John was hosing out the lion cage, an inspector from the Humane Society arrived in response to public complaints. John's housemate directed the inspector into the park to talk to John about the complaints. John was furious. He raged at the inspector, demanding to know who had complained. With the smoothness born of long practice, the inspector told him that it was not policy to reveal the identity of complainants. The conversation ended with John being handed an order, written under the Prevention of Cruelty to Animals Act, 1955. It directed him to clean the place up and have a vet attend to a festering sore on the male lion's ear.

Two weeks later the inspector returned. John had done nothing. He was still demanding to know the name of the complainant when the inspector motioned to two assistants, who responded by driving a box truck through the main gate. With the inspector on the running board, the vehicle was driven to the lion's cage.

John, beside himself with rage, watched as the male lion was driven into the smaller sleeping cage and the sliding door closed with the cable mechanism. A gun modified to shoot tranquillizer darts was produced and loaded. Within seven minutes the male lion, snoring loudly, was hoisted into a travelling crate, loaded in the truck and driven off. The inspector gravely served John with another form, stating simply that the lion was seized and would be held at the Waterloo Game Farm, three hundred miles away.

John's rage continued, unchecked and seething, until the following week, then it exploded when a bill for the previous week's exercise arrived by registered letter. Four hundred and forty dollars. John vowed he'd be damned if he'd pay such a sum and he ignored the bill. Ten days later, a note arrived by ordinary mail telling him his lion had been sold to pay the costs. The sale had raised three hundred dollars, the letter informed him, one hundred and forty remained outstanding.

While John was pondering this assault on his fortune, he heard shouts from the hippo pool. There he found a teacher smacking an eleven-year-old boy, one of a school group on a reduced-rate visit. The hippo just looked puzzled.

On persuading the teacher to desist, John learned the reason for her assault on the boy. Finding himself with visitors, the hippo had, as usual, opened his mouth, inviting his company to fill it with the peanuts and stale bread sold by John at the gate for that express purpose. This lad, having no peanuts or bread, had thrown in a plastic beach ball.

Horrified, stopping only to kick at the boy, John leapt into the pool, and chased the hippo up its ramp and into its pen. By using a broom handle as a pry-bar, he managed to open the great mouth that resembled nothing so much as a huge mechanical shovel. But no beach ball could be seen within. The unlucky animal was already trying to digest it.

The cowed school class was hastily herded back into their yellow bus, uncertain what the panic was all about. John phoned his vet. Shocked, the vet told him to load the beast on some suitable vehicle and take it at once to the school of veterinary medicine at Guelph.

"What's all that going to cost?" asked John.

"I've no idea," replied the vet, "but I do know the hippo's good as dead if you don't."

"But they've never worked on a hippo before. Why don't they come here? It would be an experience for them," John suggested.

Speechless with frustration, as he usually was in his conversations with John, the vet quietly but firmly put down the phone.

John walked back to the hippo pool carrying a pint bottle of mineral oil. By throwing a few peanuts at its nose, he persuaded the hippo to open its enormous mouth. Risking the amputation of a hand at least, John inserted his arm to the elbow between the large ivory tusks and poured in the mineral oil.

Four hours later the hippo pool was heavy with manure, but no plastic beach ball ever appeared. Over the next few days the animal grew steadily weaker and thinner. The hay, carrots, onions and other vegetables beloved by the hippo went untouched. On the morning of the fourth day the hippo floated dead in its filthy pool.

The Humane Society inspector reappeared just as John, with a block and tackle and a tow truck, was beaching the body of the dead hippo. He spoke to John gently.

"How did it die?"

"It swallowed a beach ball," grunted John as he undid the chain around the hippo's leg.

"What vet attended it?"

"None, they wouldn't come," replied John.

"They couldn't do much here," observed the inspector. "Why didn't you ship it to Guelph? They could have saved it."

"Cost too much." Ignoring the ominous silence, John went on. "Listen, why don't you go catch someone beating a dog?"

At this juncture, Megalo, the noisome local dead-stock-removal man, arrived with his closed steel-bodied wagon. Without a word he opened the back and brought out the long steel winch cable. Apart from the pathetic carcass of a little dead foal, the rear of the truck yawned empty.

The dead hippo was winched aboard and the truck drove off with the inspector following. He was joined later by the vet John had spoken to. They arrived together at Megalo's smelly dismembering shed. There, as they stood in their rubber boots and overalls, the gas-inflated hippo belly was hacked open. Yards of intestines were removed. The vet took over, groping around inside. The dead-stock man and his helpers watched as the vet retrieved the beach ball. The inspector photographed the entire proceedings, including the beach ball, made notes, conferred with the vet and drove away. The vet was left alone, still angry. Then he too went away.

Back at the zoo, the inspector walked up on John while he was cleaning out the monkeys.

"I've just come from a post-mortem examination of the hippo," he said without announcing himself. "It died of bowel stoppage. A beach ball was blocking its gut."

"Yes, I know all that," replied John, a little slowly. He looked up. "Why didn't you come help me with it? The vet wouldn't come."

"It's not my job to do that, and the vet couldn't do anything here," the inspector said just as slowly, "but I understand you were advised to send it to Guelph, and you didn't. What you did constitutes willful neglect. You will be charged with failing to provide suitable and adequate care for the hippopotamus, contrary to Section 402 of the Criminal Code. Have you anything to say? You aren't obliged to, but whatever you say will be taken down in writing and may be used as evidence."

For perhaps twenty seconds John stared speechlessly at the inspector. Then he ran into his workshop office. When he reappeared he was carrying the .308 heavy rifle he kept for escaped lions. Pointing it at the inspector, he shouted, "Get out, get out, I've had enough!" Very carefully and deliberately, the inspector walked backwards away from John to his car. He did not leave, however, but sat in the car watching John while talking into his radio, giving information and instructions. Then he climbed out of the car and walked back towards John calmly, no expression on his face. John, after a pause, began to run at him brandishing the .308. Just then two OPP officers arrived. They strode up to John and confiscated the rifle. He was arrested and charged with a second offence, pointing a firearm.

John pleaded guilty to the rifle charge and not guilty of "failing to care" for the hippo. The inspector and veterinarian told their respective stories, showed their photographs and produced the beach ball in its transparent plastic bag.

The judge wasted no time in finding John guilty. "You are not a wicked man," the judge observed, "but you are wasteful and unable to take the best advice given you." On the charge of pointing a firearm, you are fined five hundred dollars. On the charge of neglect, I am placing you on two years' probation, and a condition of that probation will be that you have a vet examine all your animals monthly and abide by his instruction."

At this point John interrupted the judge. "Now see here, Your Honour, that's likely to be expensive!"

"Not half as expensive as being brought back here," observed His Honour.

John subsided, mumbling to himself. On his way out of the courtroom he hissed at the inspector, "Next time I shoot first time."

Summer arrived in a push-up of green, and tourists called at the little zoo. But they were appalled by the filthy state of the paddocks and pens, and they left. Then their friends and acquaintances gave the place a miss. Finally no one came. In time, complaints again reached the Humane Society via the local Chamber of Commerce, the Provincial MPP, the Ministry of Tourism and the OPP.

And so it happened, one sunny afternoon, that a plain blue station wagon arrived outside the zoo gate. A sturdy-looking, well-made man of middle age and medium height climbed out of the vehicle. He did not smile as the previous inspector had done, he just glowered in the direction of John and his buildings. John sensed he represented officialdom and braced himself for what he feared would be a battle of some kind.

The man approached John as he stood in his workshop doorway.

"Are you the proprietor?" he asked in a flat English North Country voice.

John nodded.

"I am from the Humane Society. I'm going to look at your animals." He walked past John in the direction of the monkey row.

John ran in front of him. "Stop, I forbid you."

The man stopped. He removed his hands from behind his back and grasped the lapels of his corduroy jacket. "I've a search warrant, and if you obstruct me you'll be arrested," he growled, and continued his slow march.

John grasped the inspector by his coat collar and one arm. The inspector slipped out of the coat, turned, grasped John by his own collar and tie, and upended him into a puddle. Then he recovered his coat, put it on and continued his promenade. John picked himself up, dripping with water. He was shaking with rage and humiliation. Here he was on his own property and this grim little tank of a man had walked in on him and stood him on his head in a puddle. It was too much.

He ran to his workshop. There, on the hatrack, stood his .308 rifle, restored by the court. Pulling it from its rack, he checked to see that cartridges were in the magazine. He ran to his pickup truck, threw the rifle onto the seat, started the engine, pushed the gearshift and roared off in pursuit of the new inspector. He found him at the lion's cage. The inspector looked up as John slid to a halt.

"Oh, back are you?" he said, as John seemed at a loss for words. "I'm glad of that. This place is a mess. Do you know how to use a broom and shovel? You'd better learn."

John pulled the rifle from the cab and worked the bolt, pushing a live round into the breach of the gun. Before he could level it, however, he found it had been grasped by its barrel and twisted upwards. As a large, polished brogue shoe landed in his groin, he let the rifle go. It described an arc and landed on the side of his head. He lay half stunned. When after some time he recovered himself, he saw his rifle, minus its bolt, leaning against a tree. His hands, he discovered, were handcuffed behind him. His shoelaces were tied together.

The inspector said nothing, but grabbed John's clothing under the armpits, lifted him to his feet, and propelled him into the cab of his own truck. The man added the rifle to the truck now containing John. John was driven to the nearest OPP detachment and charged again with pointing a firearm.

The trial was held three weeks later. This time John went to the expense of hiring a local lawyer for his defence. It didn't help. He was found guilty and remanded in custody for two weeks for a psychiatric report. Following this, he was fined five hundred dollars, an order was made prohibiting him from owning a firearm for two years, and his probation was extended for a further year. His lawyer's bill came to seven hundred dollars and, even worse, the hated Humane Society was directed by the court to supervise the welfare of his animals.

From then on, things went into a decline. His lady friend left, unwilling to try to cope with his drinking. The monkeys picked up some obscure disease and all but the old crab-eating monkey died. For company, poor John was left with the oldest and smelliest primate of the lot—besides himself.

Winter set in quickly that year. It seemed as if the trees were their glorious red for only two days, then suddenly white with snow. The seaway froze and no visitors came. For John it was a quiet, lonely winter warmed by malt products and punctuated by visits from Humane Society inspectors. John did not always see the visitors themselves, but he knew from the large, measured footprints he found in the snow that his remaining animals had been under scrutiny.

By late winter John was aware he himself was ill. It was nothing he could actually define, but rather a feeling that something inside him was malfunctioning. Diagnosis might have been easier if he could have abstained for several days. As it was, several hours was the best he could manage. One morning he collapsed and passed out in the bathroom while sitting on the toilet. On regaining consciousness, he noted with alarm there was blood in the toilet.

He went without delay to a doctor he knew. The doctor cleaned him up, stopped the bleeding and killed the pain. He also took several samples of tissue and blood. John soon learned he had advanced and terminal cancer. By Easter he was admitted to the hospital to stay. About that time the grizzly bear escaped.

Leah and Marvin Goldblatt from Yonkers, New York, had never been to Canada before. Their expectations of Hollywood's *Rose Marie* country were completely fulfilled as they drove west along Highway 2, for there, shuffling along, was a real grizzly bear. It was John's escapee.

"Oh, look, Marvin," exclaimed Leah. "We've only been in Canada twenty minutes and here's this lovely bear. Right on the roadside too!"

"Why don't you throw it a wiener or something?" said Marvin, trying to hold his Datsun in a straight line, slow down and have a look at the bear, all at the same time. Reaching into the picnic basket, Leah took two cooked kosher wieners and threw them toward the bear, who promptly licked them up and almost without pausing reached the car and thrust her brown wedgeshaped head through the open window. By some miracle of car control and gymnastics, Marvin stopped the car, Leah climbed over the gearshift, and they escaped out of the driver's door. The bear, trapped in the window opening, shook her head twice and the door came off.

Stopping only to see the bear wearing their car door like an Elizabethan ruff, the Goldblatts ran. While they were recounting their experience to a passing motorist, the bear tore the seats out of their clean little car and ransacked their picnic basket. The Goldblatts were deposited at the nearest OPP headquarters, where they told their story.

Corporal Angus MacStravick had been hoping for a quiet Easter Friday in order to catch up on his official correspondence. His hopes were shattered by the Goldblatts' arrival and the recital of events. Some twenty minutes later, he had assembled his three available men and was trying to head the bear back into John's park. The bear entered the fringe of the bush bordering the highway readily enough, but then she vanished.

MacStravick and his men, trying to keep each other under observation, were nervous enough wading through the dead ferns, but when the bear erupted behind them with a crash of dead twigs and loud "woofs" it was too much. They ran into the park and shut themselves in an empty pen. The bear patrolled on the outside, watching them with mean, distrustful eyes.

The policemen in turn watched the bear performing sentry on the pen they were using as a haven. The bear eyed them all the while she stalked. It was obvious she was hungry. After some moments the junior constable had an idea. He had sandwiches in his cruiser, cut and packed by his loving wife of three months. If he could make it to the cruiser, he could return and throw his sandwiches into the bear's empty cage nearby. With any luck the bear would run into her old cage and, *voilà*, she would be caught. Since it was the best idea anyone had, everyone agreed to the plan.

Fortunately, the young officer was twenty-two years of age, slim and a good runner. While MacStravick and the others provided diversion, he made his way over the top of the pen, through the bush fringe and onto the roadway. He seized his brown bag of tuna-fish with mayonnaise sandwiches and returned to the others, slowly and quietly.

He also had had the sense to radio district headquarters from the car and to have taken the 12-gauge riot shotgun from it.

Returning very carefully through the aspen bush, he saw the bear still marching up and down outside the pen that, until lately, had held two wallabies. Now it held three policemen. The young officer timed his run, dropping bits of sandwich as he went, until he arrived breathless and sweaty outside the bear's own empty cage. As he undid the spring clip holding the door shut, he glimpsed the bear advancing on him, licking up pieces of sandwich as she came.

He held out the remainder of his sandwiches until the bear was seven feet from him, then, flicking them into the empty cage, he ducked behind the open door. The bear ran in, and slamming the door shut, the officer secured it with the clip. His comrades cheered.

They all crowded around the hole through which the bear had originally escaped, and the young officer fired two shots into the soft earth in front of the hole. The bear retreated to the far end of the cage. Leaving two men on guard, MacStravick sped back to his detachment office. By now it was dark and close to seven o'clock.

In my house, supper was over and my wife, daughter and a couple of old friends from Ottawa were relaxing with coffee, brandy and After Eights. The phone rang. It was MacStravick.

"Good evening, Sir! How are you tonight?" MacStravick asked in a friendly way.

"Full of supper," I said.

"I'm sorry to bother you," MacStravick went on, "but we have an escaped grizzly bear. Can you come down and do something about it? It's from the Seaway Zoo."

"Well, not tonight," I replied. "You see, I'll have to get a crate, a truck and some help, and I can't do that before nine. Then I have to get down there. First plane in the morning is the best I can do."

"We're trying to keep it in the cage it escaped from,"

MacStravick continued. "What should we do if it tries to get out again?"

"Fire moves them, Corporal. Fire some gasoline, oil or road flares, and get a vet lined up! I'll be there about eleven tomorrow morning." I hung up, excused myself to our guests, and began to make arrangements.

When I finally arrived at one o'clock the next day, the members of the detachment had made an enormous dent in their fifth crate of road flares. Burned-out road flares hung from the gaping front of the cage like grapes at a Niagara wine festival. In front of the hole stood a diminutive woman constable fingering a shotgun almost as big as herself. When relieved of her post by MacStravick, she vanished with alacrity, taking her shotgun with her.

There were also signs of my arrangements. A hired three-ton truck with a lifting platform had arrived, driven by a junior inspector from a game farm in Cambridge—a four-hour journey for him. Bolt cutters had been brought, in addition to a gun that fired tranquillizer darts, some one-and-a-half-inch nylon rope, a three-inch rope sling and some tie-down ropes. Now all that was needed was a veterinarian to provide the necessary drugs.

The police had found one vet who had agreed to accompany them, only to cry off when he was told it was a grizzly bear they were dealing with. Two other vets also declined on the grounds they knew nothing about bears.

"We'll have to have a vet from somewhere," I said when told there was no vet standing by. "Otherwise one or two of us will get hurt." The silent group of constables, gripping their *Fabrique National* semi-auto rifles, mutely affirmed the bear's fate should she try any further to escape.

"Perhaps we can get Doctor Collins," said a senior constable. "He has a general practice. What drugs do you require?"

"Rompun and Ketomyn. Don't tell him what it's for, just ask him if he's got any."

The good Dr. Collins, D.V.M., was telephoned and asked to be ready with the drugs. MacStravick and I set off in the familiar black-and-white car to the vet's residence. Dr. Collins appeared on the doorstep in his shirt sleeves and carpet slippers.

"Have you some Rompun and Ketomyn, Doctor?" I asked.

"Sure," replied the vet. "It's right here in my bags. The boys at the station just asked if I had some."

"Good," grunted MacStravick, "come with us." He grasped one arm, I grasped the other and the vet's bag, and together we hijacked the vet from his own doorstep.

"Now, what's all this about?" he demanded as the cruiser roared off. "We're having an early supper today. I have to attend a church musical evening, and I haven't even told my wife where I've gone."

"Don't worry, Doc, you won't be ten minutes. All the inspector here wants is a little help with a grizzly bear. Right?" grinned MacStravick.

"Grizzly bear, grizzly bear, don't know anything about 'em!"

"Don't worry," I soothed, "all I need is eighteen cc's of Rompun and Ketomyn. Ten and eight, well mixed, I know the dosage."

"Well, I don't," pouted the vet. "I'll supply it and mix it, and then I'm going. I'm having nothing to do with this."

The eighteen cubic centimetres of drugs were measured out. They filled a ten-cc dart and a five-cc dart. Three remained in the syringe, which was held in reserve.

"That's it, I'm off," exclaimed the vet when he had measured out the dosage.

"Please stay," I asked. "You can sit in the police car, where you'll be safe."

"Damned if I ever get caught in a thing like this again."

I took out the Palmer-Capchur gun, pushed the dart up the barrel with the adapter, selected the low-power charge and looked about me. The bolt cutters stood against the cage with the three-inch sling, the nylon rope was run out and across the lane, over the ridge and onto the road shoulder, and the travelling crate with its two sliding doors in the up position stood nearby. The nylon rope led through it and was tied to a spring on the police car.

The tranquillizer gun gave a dull crack and the bear tore at the dart that was well stuck into its left buttock. Within seconds, a further shot placed the second dart in the right buttock.

"Darts fired, sixteen eleven hours and thirty-two seconds," chanted Stu, the junior inspector who had accompanied me, with practised ease as he wrote it in his book. Everyone studied the bear, who was now biting and tearing at her rear.

She caught one alloy dart in her teeth and tossed it, by then flat and misshapen, out of the cage. Seven minutes later, the animal was staggering around its cage like a summer drunk on a beach, but she simply would not lie down. "We'll have to give her the lot," I observed finally. "You guys will have to distract her."

As I spoke, I took a worn and battered corn broom from the cab of the hired truck and walked to the cage door.

Stu and his assistant waved a piece of rag inside the cage between the bars as, corn broom in my left hand and syringe in my right, I was helped through the cage door by a policeman. Inside the police car the vet had shut his eyes, evidently wishing himself elsewhere. Going behind the staggering animal, I managed to smack the flat of the broom against the great wedge-shaped head. Slowly the round, tufted ears flicked, as the head turned and the huge pale-yellow fangs snapped at the stubby corn bristles. At that point I pressed the plunger of the syringe and its contents were quickly injected into the right buttock muscles. I stepped back smartly against the cage door, which opened. The grizzly took two floundering steps in pursuit of me and fell flat on her face. Everyone relaxed.

Stu's assistant had been waiting, poised with the bolt cutters on the cage front. When the bear fell down, I said, "Go, Leslie," and Leslie fell to work like a demented tailor, snipping away at the chain-link cage front with the bolt cutters. The vet was meanwhile driven back home.

Three minutes later, the cage front was folded up like a vast transparent tent flap. The three-inch sling was eased round the bear, which by now was snoring. She rolled easily onto it. The long rope was tied on and the driver of the police car took up the slack rope. Slowly, ever so slowly at first, the eight-hundred-pound bear was eased round and forward in the cage.

We three Humane Society men lifted up the great head and forearms over the cage lip and the fat rib section followed. Down the bank went the sleeping body in its sling, across the lane, over the ridge and finally into the crate. The quick release knot was pulled and the long rope came away. While we rocked the heavy beast, the sling was eased out from beneath her. The doors were slammed down and locked. Next we rocked the crate onto the truck platform, raised it, pushed it inside the truck, and tied it down. As we did so, the bear woke up.

By truck and Air Canada, the driver and crew made their way back to the Society farm at West Gwillimbury. The truck arrived at one-thirty in the morning, having limped the last fifty miles with a badly slipping clutch.

The next day, the truck was towed to the game farm and the bear was unloaded. The day after that, the crew was back at the zoo removing a pair of llamas, three crazy mules, a pony, a nasty tempered buffalo and the remaining monkey, now the sole primate resident of John's establishment.

Apart from the buffalo chasing Stu into a cold pond, the removal was fairly routine. The next day, Easter Tuesday, we all went back to normal duties, and gave thanks.

THE
PET
MOTEL

WE RECEIVED COMPLAINTS ABOUT THE PEPE PET Motel and Boutique on a fairly regular basis. Our man at Church Lake would pay visits to it, and the place would be cleaned up, only to lapse soon after into its usual state of neglect.

The problem was in Northern Ontario. We seldom received any other complaints from the district surrounding Church Lake, and the cost of return air fare for one complaint, which might well prove unfounded, was an expense we simply couldn't afford. The efforts of our man at Church Lake—the town itself two hours' drive from the motel—had to serve for the regular motel complaints. He was a church worker by profession, and while conscientious and knowledgeable, he was not a forceful personality. This fact had augmented our problem for some time before, by chance, it came to my attention.

The human cause of the problem took the form of a Sylvia DeForge, proprietor of the motel premises. Sylvia, it was reported, sometimes left dogs chained out on her front lawn for days on end, and although she fed them, she did *not* clean up after them. The animals lay about in their own filth for days because Sylvia just "didn't get around to it."

After one of the occasions reported by our man in Church Lake, we were assured that Sylvia herself was a very clean person. It seemed that the dogs were simply of little concern to her.

"But surely," I reasoned on the phone, "if she does this for a living, it's in her own interest to keep the place clean. It doesn't add up."

"It beats me too," our man agreed. "She's always polite, she offers me tea, the house is clean. I can't understand her."

We terminated that telephone conversation, and Sylvia DeForge, as so many times before, slipped from my mind.

It was at this point that we had the Great Canadian Wagon Train inflicted on us. Every day we had to check on the condition of the horses as they slowly trekked northwest. Soon they were out of commuting distance from Toronto. Shortly after that they were out of commuting distance of any of our shelters. Sooner or later someone would have to fly north to check the horses. "Someone" once more turned out to be me. And while I was there, it was decided, I might as well first check out the situation at the motel.

Our man at Church Lake met me at the airport. He was a small, worried-looking man, deathly afraid of making some horrendous error that would saddle him and the Society with an expensive lawsuit. The flight had created in me an irritated attitude, so my manner did little to reassure him. He tried not to look horrified when a nasty little boy in the airport pointed at me and announced to his mother, "That's the man that told me to go outside and play when we were on the plane, Mum." His mother gave me the desperate look of a woman who has a child beyond her control, and I made nice noises to our man from Church Lake. At least I tried.

We drove in silence to the original part of the old Northern Ontario town. We passed the convenience stores now operated by Korean emigrants, the laundromats, and the closed butcher shops that were victims of the supermarket chains. We halted in front of a modest bungalow with an overgrown lawn. It was located on the south side of the street. Behind the small house, a rusty steel building contained the sound of barking and declared itself as the kennel. A faded signboard on the lawn announced: PEPE PET MOTEL AND BOUTIQUE.

"Ah well, let's get to it," I muttered as I climbed down from the four-wheel-drive van.

Our man in Church Lake followed reluctantly. I rang the bell and while I waited I looked over the premises. The house was pink, the door was pink but outlined with wine-coloured lines, the shutters were wine, and so were the downspouts. It was a distinctive house. Unmistakable. You couldn't miss it even with dim directions for finding it.

I was braced for a hostile reception. There was none. There was no answer at all to my persistent ringing and knocking.

"Ask next door, see if they know where she is."

"Right," my assistant said, happy to remove himself from the front of the pink house and probable unpleasantness.

I myself went to the house in the opposite direction.

"Good morning," I began, smiling at the sour-looking, cigarette-smoking elderly lady who came to the door.

"I'm not buying anything today," she grumbled hoarsely.

"I'm not selling anything," I said. "I'm from the Humane Society." I handed her my identification card.

She looked at the reverse side of my card, which had my description on it. She studied it for a moment, then handed it back.

"I don't know anyone called Hazel," she wheezed.

I went to the next house, then on to several others.

By inquiring of the neighbours generally, we discovered that Mrs. DeForge had gone on holiday, Mrs. Deforge had gone to Toronto on business, Mrs. DeForge was in Montreal learning business methods, Mrs. DeForge was in London, England, and Mrs. DeForge was in Winnipeg learning the body rub business.

It was plain Mrs. DeForge was not home. We went to

the kennel building, which was unlocked. Two small boys were going through the motions of cleaning out the runs of the seven small dogs confined there. Most of the fecal matter was simply being spread around on the wet floor. The entire steel building dripped with condensation. All of the dogs had kennel cough. This was not an ideal environment for anyone, especially small boys.

Leaving my new friend to remove the seven dogs, I went back to the house. A small puppy-like yapping came from within. It was loudest outside a bolted side window. There was nothing else for it, I'd have to get a search warrant to investigate properly.

During business hours it's usual to find a justice of the peace in the local court building or, failing that, a police station. I'm speaking of urban conventions. In country districts, on the other hand, I've obtained warrants almost anywhere. I once got one signed on the fuel tank of a tractor while the J.P. interrupted his spring plowing to grant my request. In this particular town the J.P. had a small office in the basement adjoining the bookstore. He was a short, fat man with thick spectacles that seemed too small for his large, moon-like face. He nodded perfunctorily when I stated my business.

"Come in," he said gruffly, motioning with his head to the musty, book-lined cubbyhole. He eyed me for some minutes.

"What police department are you with?" he asked.

"I'm not with a police department. I'm from the Humane Society." I produced my "information form," made out in duplicate on the battered typewriter I had located in the police waiting room. I also produced the completed warrant, also filled out on one of our special forms. I had brought some with me.

He held the information form up to within six inches of his thick spectacles and read it slowly and carefully, his tongue licking his thin lips as they silently formed the words. Next he picked up the warrant, treating it in a like manner.

"I can't accept these," he said at length. "Not correct."

"What's wrong?" I was already exasperated.

"Wrong forms," he stated, laying them down with finality upon his desk.

"No, sir, they are forms one and two, as specified in the Act."

"What Act is that?" he enquired with a faint smile.

"Why, the Provincial Society for the Prevention of Cruelty to Animals Act," I replied.

"I've never heard of it." He sounded a man on firm ground.

"Here," I said, rummaging in my briefcase, "here's a copy. The forms are set out on page nine at the end."

For the next fifteen minutes he read my copy of the Act from first page to last.

"Very interesting," he concluded, "but it's not in the revised statutes, so it can't be correct."

"Yes, it is," I countered. "It's in the Supplements."

"Ah, I don't have the Supplements. Can't help you I'm afraid." He turned away, opened a drawer, brought out a tuna sandwich and began eating his lunch.

Feeling baffled and a little like Alice in Wonderland, I backed out of the office. The Crown attorney was unavailable. His secretary, who plainly didn't care much for strange persons like myself, had no idea if they had any Supplements. "You'll have to wait," she told me. I waited.

Twenty minutes later the harassed Crown counsel bustled along the corridor with an attendant pack of defence lawyers, newspaper reporters and detectives keeping station around him. He walked right past me into his office. The entourage went with him.

"Will you tell him I'd like to see him on this matter?" I asked the secretary.

"He'll be out soon enough, you can tell him yourself."

Ah, me mother told me there would be days like this. I walked past her and into the office. Not one of them took the slightest notice of me. I walked over to the bookcase while they talked back and forth. I couldn't see the red-backed Supplements volume anywhere. I walked across to the knot of people surrounding the prosecutor, leaned through them and said, "I say, have you a Supplements you can lend me?"

"Sorry, Judge Hogan's borrowed mine. Somebody stole his." He didn't even look up.

The judges' chambers were farther along the corridor. I looked for Judge Hogan's name. I found it. He was out and so was his secretary. Next door was Judge Wiley. His secretary was a calm-looking woman of about forty.

"I'm trying to locate a copy of the Provincial Statutes Supplements. Do you have a law library where I could locate one perhaps?"

She looked at me, puzzled. It seemed I had the correct English but my appearance—blue overalls, baseball cap and overshoes—didn't quite fit my request.

"I'm from the Humane Society," I added by way of explanation.

She nodded with her mouth slightly open. There was no doubt she took me for some sort of literate lunatic.

"We haven't got one. Why don't you try Judge Fineberg down the hall."

Judge Fineberg's secretary was absent from the reception room. The door to the judge's room was ajar. I put my eye to the crack. I could see no one, so I pushed it slowly open and walked in. The desk was empty. To the right of it stood a large bookcase. On the lower shelves, at the extreme right, were the Supplements. I walked across the clean, soft-pile broadloomed carpet. There it was, the volume I needed: 1955–56. I picked it up. A loud snore almost caused me to drop it. I turned carefully, holding the precious volume to my breast. I saw a chesterfield against the far wall that had been beyond my line of vision when I entered. Sprawled on it was His Honour, sound asleep. They were a long nine steps to the door, but I made it, clutching the purloined Supplements volume.

Outside in the corridor I allowed myself a silent whoop of victory and skipped down the three flights of stairs to the grubby basement room of the J.P. He was in the process of locking the door before he went for his post-prandial walk.

"Let me show you this Supplement," I said, blocking his exit. He looked mildly surprised. I was panting slightly as I showed him the volume.

"Where'd you get that?" he exclaimed. "I've never seen one."

"Judge Fineberg loaned it to me. He says you've no grounds for refusing to sign my warrant." I paused. "You know what that means," I added in what I hoped was a sinister tone.

"Yes, yes." He was holding the volume up to his short-sighted eyes. "Umm," he intoned, "you're right." He closed the book with a snap. "But I can't think why you should be bothering Sylvy. Everyone knows Sylvy."

He signed the warrant, and I literally ran out of his basement, warrant in hand. I stopped only to place the Supplement on Judge Fineberg's "In" tray. When I returned to our man in Church Lake, he was sitting in his vehicle.

"Thought you were never coming back. Stopped for lunch, I suppose." Behind him the caged terriers wheezed and yapped.

I walked up to the pink door and turned the knob. The door was unlocked, so we walked in. A Great Dane puppy pounded away from us. The phone rang. I picked it up.

"Is that you, Sylvy?" asked a man's voice. I thought I knew the voice. "Listen, there's a guy from some Society or another coming to see you about your dogs."

"She's not here," I answered firmly.

"Damn," said the voice as the receiver clicked off.

My man had chased the Great Dane puppy into a rear room. I followed, only to find him trying to extract the pup from under a king-sized bed. The bed and a small adjoining bathroom completed the amenities of the room.

We caught the long-legged, floppy-eared pup at last, after he and my man had fought a short tug of war.

"Can't think why they'd leave all these little balloons under the bed," he said.

I looked. The "balloons" were used condoms. Clearly my churchwarden was unfamiliar with certain facts of life.

Carrying the puppy, we went back to the entrance hall. A large clothes closet held some men's coats and overshoes. Two pairs of overshoes were of size fourteen.

"Must be big men," my man observed.

The hall led to a sitting-cum-dining room with a tiled fireplace. Very handsome. Four bedrooms led off from this room. Three were small with adjoining bathrooms. One was large. It was the only one with built-in closets and good furniture. One closet held dresses and coats neatly arranged on hangers. The other held several wigs of various shades, ranging from blonde through red to black. There was something that looked to be a sort of leather swimsuit, leather gauntlet-like gloves, a black leather mask and a many-tailed whip. An assortment of straps, chains and locks were scattered on the closet floor.

"Can't think why anyone would go swimming in a leather swimsuit," the churchman said.

"You really have no idea, have you?" I asked.

"Idea of what?" he bristled.

"This place. It's a brothel. The dogs are a blind."

He was incredulous. His mouth was open, and suddenly so were his eyes.

"You mean to say I've been drinking tea in a whore house? Whatever will my wife say!"

I grinned. "Nothing, if you don't tell her. I shouldn't tell your minister either, or your deacons. They may not understand it was your duty."

He looked around at the pornographic magazines on the side tables. He thumbed through one or two as he thought over my advice. His neck went a deep red.

"Yes," he mused aloud. "After all, it was my duty."

Holding the puppy under his arm, he squared back his shoulders and marched out to his truck.

With a tack hammer I affixed to the doors the usual red-

and-white notices to the effect that we had seized the animals therein. Then I locked all the doors and windows.

"What a place, what a place," my man at Church Lake repeated as he drove me to the airport. "Just think of it. I was in there drinking tea."

"Didn't leave your overshoes, did you?" I asked.

For a minute he looked worried, then he smiled. "No fear, kept 'em on." He dropped me at the entrance to the departure lounge and rattled off back to the municipality of Church Lake.

Back in my office I waited for the abusive demanding phone call. It never arrived. The official seizure papers were returned uncollected. Mrs. DeForge, it seemed, had left the Pepe Pet Motel for good.

Thirty days later I did receive a phone call from my opposite number in the adjoining province. He needed my assistance, he explained, in disposing of an eight-foot boa constrictor and a five-foot male alligator. I recommended a reliable reptile collector. It was arranged I would meet him two days hence on the provincial border, where he would turn the reptiles over to me for transfer to the Ontario sanctuary.

So it was that I went to collect the exotic animals and place them in their new home.

"Tell me how you came by these?" I asked.

He chuckled as he prepared to tell his story. It was short but unforgettable.

"You see, we were called by the provincial police one night. They had raided a nightclub in the Laurentians. Women with no clothes on were presenting the show. One of them was dancing with the snake I gave you."

"And the other?"

"Oh, oh," his face twisted with embarrassment. "How shall I say? You see, she was under the alligator. A Miss DeForge—from your part of the country. She's doing nine months for indecent exhibition."

When I returned to my office I forwarded the seizure documents to her prison address. I never received a reply.

TROUBLE
AT THE
BACK END

MY FRIEND JAMES IS A VETERINARY SURGEON, AN EX-
cellent one, specializing in horses. On one occasion James
and I had spent a pleasant evening sampling a new export
product from Scotland. We had decided it was acceptable
but dreadfully overpriced. After several snorts of the stuff
we vowed we'd write personally and tell both the provincial and federal finance ministers just what a disservice to
mankind they were doing by taxing it out of existence.

During the conversation, James had confided in me that
a new account he had was giving him trouble. It was a
stable with a large number of stallions. James's assistant
was not really up to holding the high-spirited horses while
James gave them their injections.

"Don't worry, James," I said patronizingly, "you can
always call me."

"Can I really?" he asked brightly.

"Of course," I said. The "of course" was the result of
several drams of Scotland's gift to the world.

"I'll remember that!" shouted James from his front door
as I bade him goodnight and strolled off home.

And indeed he did. At precisely six-ten the next morning my phone rang. It was James calling on me for help
with one of his accounts. He would pick me up in twenty
minutes. Trying to wash the creases of sleep and time from
my face, I quietly cursed myself for having offered my

services the previous evening. I pulled on some clothes and had just enough time to gulp down a scalding mug of coffee before James's van halted at the door. I climbed into the vehicle, and we roared off almost before I had sat down.

"Where's the fire?" I asked.

"It's a horse in a bad way, by the sound of it. They called my number at five after six. Sounds like a monumental bowel stoppage. I'll have to get my arm up, and I'll need the head well held. In view of your offer last night, I thought your coming with me would be an ideal solution to the problem."

Fumes of "Dirty Kilt"—as I thought of it this morning —were still addling my brain. I hunched myself down in the well-upholstered captain's chair of James's van and tried not to think about my fragile state of health vis-à-vis the activity to come.

Have you ever ridden in a practising country vet's vehicle? It has a smell all its own. He usually carries large supplies of just about every medicinal aid he's likely to need. The tools alone make a long list: pulling chains and cranks for calves that stick at birth; a tool that looks like a bolt cutter but is, in fact, a Burrdizzo castrator for calves; a lasso with a breakaway metal hondo that permits instant release; a large post-mortem knife; pull-on rubber boots; disinfectant; a pail and a long-handled scrubbing brush to wash equipment between calls.

The vehicle slowed and I opened my eyes. We were pulling into a red-brick-walled yard, the back yard of a police station.

"Where are we?" I asked.

"Eighty-Eighth Division. It's one of their horses that has the problem."

James parked and we both alighted, a little stiff. I looked at my watch. It was seven-fifteen.

We walked up to the stable block. James, of course, was known. I was introduced, and accompanied by two constables of the mounted detachment we went into the stables.

There were ten horses in wide standing stalls and one in a box stall.

The problem was with a horse named Caspian. He was what in English circles would be called a "heavyweight hunter, up to eighteen stone." From his appearance and physical conformation I judged him to be a Belgian draft horse bred to a Trakhaner or Swedish warmblood, or perhaps a Hanoverian. Whatever his ancestry, he was a big lump of a horse, but elegant. I would have loved to have been astride him on a sunny November morning in West Berkshire, or Leicester on a good day. That horse had conformation and presence. Charisma almost.

He stood in the end standing stall. The problem was what was behind him. The ten horses, during the course of the night hours, each normally excreted perhaps thirty pounds of manure. It accumulated behind them and it was the duty of the "early turn" stable officer to remove it. At six a.m. he had signed in. Two minutes later he had called the sergeant, who had called James, who had called me. The droppings behind Caspian were gargantuan for a horse. Each must have weighed ten pounds. James studied Caspian's rear end. Caspian, turning his head, studied James.

"Tell me," said James, "when was this horse fed last and what was he fed?"

The sergeant consulted his daily sheet. "He was fed five pounds of bran/oats mixture at five-thirty p.m. and ten pounds of hay at nine p.m., before the 'late turn' stable man went off duty."

"So he wasn't fed anything from nine p.m. onwards—that's true?"

"That's true as far as we know, sir," replied the sergeant.

James studied Caspian again. He lifted Caspian's tail, carefully inspecting what lay beneath. Nothing seemed unusual. James rubbed his chin. He turned to me.

"What do you make of this?" he asked anxiously.

"Let's take one of these droppings outside and examine it," I suggested.

"Right," he agreed.

Commandeering the detachment wheelbarrow and dung fork, I picked up a fair specimen, dumped it in the barrow and wheeled it outside. James took out his long-handled scrubbing brush and dealt the lump a sharp rap. A few of the golden-brown threads fell away, but in the main the mass held together. James now brought out his heavy armour, his post-mortem knife, which is something like a heavy butcher's knife. The razor-sharp blade sliced through the cannon ball of dung. We examined the flat side of the golden sphere.

"Good knife," I commented.

"First class," said James. "The wife gets me to do our big roasts and Christmas turkey with it."

We worked earnestly at the orb of recycled grass before us. We identified masticated hay, with the odd undigested grain of oats here and there, exactly what the horses had been fed the previous evening. As I wheeled the barrow and contents to the manure pit, I had an uneasy feeling I was being watched. I propped the barrow against the wall by the manure pit, in the time-honoured way of stablekeepers since the seventeenth century.

"We'd better have him outside," said James when I returned.

The constable promptly slapped a lead-shank on Caspian's well-made, oiled-leather halter. He walked him out into the yard with the marked clip-clop of a shod horse on hard ground.

James went to his van, shrugged off his sports jacket and pulled on overalls and boots. Last of all, he pulled on a long, transparent plastic glove and sleeve. I tugged my stout leather gloves on and unswivelled my rope and chain lead-shank. I also took out James's horse-twitch. This is a wooden sledgehammer shaft with a noose of soft cotton sash-cord at one end. The horse's upper lip is inserted into the twisted cotton noose, and by increasing the pressure, it is kept there. It hurts, true enough, but it acts as a counter-irritant and keeps the horse's mind off worse things.

I put the lead-shank chain over Caspian's nose, picked up a handful of his ample upper lip and imprisoned it in the cotton noose. Caspian cocked one ear forward and the other back, but otherwise remained passive.

"O.K., James, I've got him."

"Fine," grunted James as he carefully inserted his soaped arm up Caspian's rectal cavity.

The horse did a little tap-dancing with his front feet, too near to mine for comfort. I applied the twitch a little tighter and told him what a good boy he was. The police looked on impassively. I still had the uneasy feeling someone was watching us.

"There's nothing I can find wrong there," muttered James as he withdrew his reeking right arm.

He carefully peeled off the glove, inside out so as not to soil anything or anyone. We were interrupted at this point by a stylish black car entering the yard. A tall, heavy man climbed out. All three policemen stood to attention and saluted.

"Superintendent Chisholm," said the largest one.

"This horse going to live, or shall we have him put down now?" Superintendent Chisholm barked.

James replied reasonably that he could see no reason for destruction at this early stage. I slackened off the twitch and handed Caspian over to one of the constables.

"Well, I've sent for the dead-stock man anyway," Superintendent Chisholm told us. "Can't have the poor beast suffering, eh?"

Caspian didn't look as if he were suffering. He looked hungry; and the remaining horses sounded angry. It was now forty minutes past their feed time. The sergeant and constable went inside and the whinnying, snorts and door-kicking subsided. The steady crunch-crunch of oats and bran being ground by back teeth soon came to our ears. Caspian, however, continued to whinny and snort, still among the hungry.

"James," I said, "let's feed him and see what sort of droppings he moves, while we're here."

"Capital idea," said James. "Let's give him a sloppy bran mash."

We announced our intention to the mounted staff. They bustled about, heating up an electric kettle of water and measuring out the bran. Then they discovered there was no salt on hand. I asked where salt could be found. The sergeant thought I might find some in the coffee room, in the main station.

Halfway across the yard I saw the plain, black, battered wagon of Megalo, the dead-stock removal man. The doleful-looking worker in charge opened the tailgate, ran out the steel hawser, placed his battered single-shot .22 rifle on the tailgate and stood there sharpening his sticking-and-bleeding knife. I paused in mid-stride but carried on to the canteen.

The canteen room was a pleasant place—airy, spacious, overlooking the yard. I noticed two things. The curtains were drawn and the room was full of policemen standing idly around, most of whom looked as if someone had just told them a good joke.

Picking up a full salt shaker, I nodded and strolled out. As I moved down the corridor I heard roars of laughter. I handed the salt over to the constable mixing the bran mash and motioned with my head to James, who joined me outside.

Again we looked at Caspian, who by now was telling the world he'd had no breakfast. Another stylish car drove into the yard. It was District Commander Forbes, we were told in a raw Glaswegian accent.

"What's happening lads?" he asked anxiously. "That horse is real quiet, and big enough to carry me in the Santa Claus Parade. I don't care to lose him."

We nodded in sympathy and once more moved out of earshot.

"There's something funny going on here," I said. "I don't believe that horse made those footballs at all."

"I'm of the same mind," agreed James, "but just what have we got here?"

The District Commander had entered the stable. We both heard a muffled cheer from the coffee room. Looking up out of the corner of my eye, I saw several sets of eyes peering out through chinks in the curtains.

"Let's take a walk round the yard," said James. "We may happen on the answer to this puzzle."

Hands clasped behind us, we solemnly strolled round the yard, looking behind parked cars, vans and motorcycles. In a recess by the coffee shop's side door stood a large green-painted garbage hopper. It was too high on the sides for us to see in, but by employing an empty milk crate I managed a good view of the contents. It was the usual collection of society's discards. Most of it was contained in plastic bags, good strong ones. What caught my eye was a large cardboard carton. The printing and pictures on the side proclaimed that it once had held diapers. There was no earthly reason for it to be there. Taking a deep breath, I vaulted over the garbage hopper's edge into the squelchy, smelly cargo. I threw out the carton and jumped out to join James. We both examined the carton. It was stained a deep manure-green inside. The inside corners were still wet. It smelled of manure all right, but not horse, not cow, something back in the grabbag of my mind.

"I have it!" whooped James. "It's elephant dung!"

My memory had homed in on the smell now too. "Circus, right, that's it, the smell of circus! But how, why?"

We looked at one another and then strode purposefully back towards Caspian and the company of mounted and senior officers. The horse slaughterer, cigarette-end balanced on his lip, was pulling out the heavy cable from his van, getting ready to reach Caspian's neck so he could be hauled in when shot. He had got out the hose and wet the concrete yard around the horse. "So the blood don't stick," he explained lamely.

As we strode past, a solitary policeman emerged from the canteen door and marched diagonally past us. As he reached the group of men, he did a smart eyes-left and salute, but his mouth slanted towards where the sergeant stood. "Elephant dung," he hissed as he marched by. Once outside the main gate he ran, jumped into his own private car and drove away, fast.

"What's that?" demanded the Superintendent. "Stop that man, stop him." But it was too late.

The Commander quietly hand-rolled himself a cigarette. He felt about his pockets for a match.

"Chisholm," he said carefully, "just take your sergeant-laddy and check who's in the canteen."

What followed can best be described as a minor earthquake. The building seemed to rock as many, many feet could be heard running. Doors banged, and overturned chairs and tables added to the din.

Caspian had finished his bran mash. James looked at his watch. "Hmmm, ten past eight." We waited. At eight-twenty Caspian dropped ten pounds of normal horse droppings.

"That lets us out," said James, breathing a sigh. "I guess there's no business for you," he declared, pointing to the dead-stock man, who looked like a vulture sighting a revived corpse. He hauled in his steel cable and put away the instruments of death.

District Commander Forbes walked slowly back to us, puffing at his cigarette and smiling thinly. "You know what we have here, gentlemen? A bunch of practical jokers. They had a suspect-on-premises call from the zoo about three a.m. A lot of the night shift attended. When they came back they brought that damned great box of elephant dung and dumped it behind Chisholm's best horse. He's livid, of course, but fortunately there's no harm done." However, his eyes narrowed. "Them that did it are going to pay your fees."

We drove home. I felt more robust than I had on the journey down. James seemed brighter.

"Well, Professor," I said, "that was a case well solved."

James paused. "You know, if you hadn't found that carton I don't know what I'd have done. My professional reputation was at stake over a box of elephant dung."

We arrived at his home at nine-thirty a.m. His wife had a large stack of pancakes and maple syrup for us. We suddenly discovered we were hungry.

James came over to my house that night. We had a glass or two and laughed over the day's events.

"You know," he chuckled, "I should write to the veterinary college and suggest that all students be shown the difference between horse and elephant droppings."

I agreed.

NOT
IN THE
PUBLIC
INTEREST

"THE DIRECTOR HAS SENT YOU THIS CLIPPING," SAID Helen, his secretary. "He wants to know if we have any similar cases you know of."

I took the portion of the *Groan and Wail* proffered me and read that the RCMP in rural Alberta were investigating the deaths of cattle and horses near Nanton, Brooks and Fort Macleod. In each case the animals' sex organs had been sliced cleanly off. The RCMP were baffled. There were no signs of a struggle, no tire tracks, no footprints, no traces of lethal drugs or foreign agents in the animals' blood. The newspaper report speculated that at least some of the mutilations had to do with bestiality or the rites of a satanic cult.

It was all news to me. I told Helen I'd heard of nothing like it in our territory. "Let him know if you do turn anything up," she said. "He's keen to make a press release on the subject."

I acknowledged her request and set off in my Eagle wagon to work on a survey I was conducting at the time on horses being trucked for slaughter to Owen Sound, site of Ontario's only legal horse slaughtering plant.

At midday I phoned in from a dusty, drafty call box situated outside a well-known truck stop on Highway 10. May, our receptionist, answered.

"It's the OPP in Forest Hills. They want to see you about someone cutting up a cow."

"Alive or dead?" I asked.

"They didn't say," she continued, unruffled. "Do you want the phone number? His name is MacStravick."

I noted down the phone number and succeeded in reaching the OPP in Forest Hills. Apparently MacStravick had been waiting for my call since nine-thirty that morning. I was to meet him at Hilda's at two o'clock.

Skipping lunch, I pushed the old Eagle in the direction of Forest Hills and Hilda's. I arrived with ten minutes to spare. The desire for lunch had left me. I settled for a pot of tea and a generous portion of coconut cream pie. I was munching on the pie when promptly at two Constable MacStravick marched in. He placed his order for lunch, then came and sat down at my table.

"Since you're the only fellah in here, you must be Hepworth."

Mouth full of pie, I nodded.

"It's about this cattle mutilation," he continued. "I was called to a pasture this morning, to a steer with its tongue cut out, and someone had also removed his scrotum. It's the damnedest thing you ever saw."

I savoured the last few mouthfuls of pie before drawing a breath to acknowledge this statement. MacStravick's slices of pot roast arrived on the table.

"Much blood about?" I asked matter-of-factly.

"Nooo."

"Guts hanging out of the body cavity perhaps?" I asked. MacStravick slowed his chewing. "Freshly done and all that, I take it. Body still warm?"

MacStravick ceased chewing, clutched his table napkin to his mouth and ran out to the Gents. I refilled my teacup and was stirring my tea slowly when he returned, his face a trifle pale against his navy blue uniform.

Managing to hold down the remainder of his lunch, MacStravick suggested we set off for the site of the dead steer. I agreed, and he took off in his official car. I followed behind at a more sedate pace. I'm normally a slow driver. We drove to a lonely hilltop meadow in Asprey Township, where we left the vehicles on the roadside.

I took out my camera, pulled on my rubber boots and followed the officer across the field. We strode through the damp alfalfa to a woodlot scarcely a quarter of an acre in area. The body lay on the edge of the woodlot, screened from the roadway.

"How did you find it?" I asked.

"The farmer who owns it told me," said MacStravick. "He has another job. Drives a gravel truck for the township and counts his stock on his way to and from work. This morning he was two short. He saw some crows coming up from the woodlot and walked over to find this."

I looked at the bloated carcass, now speckled with flies. I photographed it from four angles. One thing was plainly obvious, whoever had removed bits of the animal had used a very sharp knife. There was none of the lacerated tearing of a dog, wolf or bear kill. What was even more unusual, there was no sign of the cause of death. No bullet holes, no sign of violence at all. I speculated silently to myself. Had it been struck by lightning?

"I'll need an autopsy on the body," I informed the perspiring young officer. "Can you get your detachment on the radio and ask them to phone a farmer or trucker who can take this to Guelph? And we'll need a tractor and a bucket to lift it onto the truck."

I looked around at the lush untrodden grass in this continuation of the Niagara Escarpment. Immediately in front of me was the woodlot, fenced off from the meadow I was presently in. Using the 200-millimetre camera lens as a telescope, I scanned the fence line. It was unbroken. There was no trace of a gap of any kind where a beast could have forced its way through.

I dropped the camera down on my chest and looked up. A turkey vulture spiralled on a thermal high above. The species is mainly restricted to the Niagara Escarpment in Ontario. This one was circling purposefully. Using the lens again, I could make out a second large wing span joining the first. I climbed the fence and pushed my way through the woodlot. As I cleared the trees, four or five crows flew up a short distance to my right. I walked in that direction. There lay the second missing steer. The body was in a condition almost identical to that of the first one.

Once again I readied the camera. I scrawled "2" on the back of a visiting card with ballpoint ink and I propped the card on the uppermost point of the beast's shoulder. Again I took four photographs. What was baffling was that there was no trace at all as to how this body, like the other, had arrived where it lay. There were no tracks in the leaf mold of the woodlot. There was no crushed or flattened grass to mark its passage.

I rejoined my young friend at his cruiser and told him of the second body. We sat speculating until the cattle owner's brother and father arrived with a stock truck and a tractor, complete with a large bucket mounted on the front. Together we turned the bodies over into the bucket of the tractor, and by rolling them back again, eased them into the body of the truck. As we did so I noticed something hitherto hidden.

Since each body had lain right side up, I had been unable to examine the left underside. On the left shoulder of each dead animal was a blue spot about two to three inches across. It was bright blue, almost fluorescent, paint. It was as though someone had taken a tennis ball, dipped it in paint, then hurled it at the beast, striking it on the shoulder. The impact would have flattened the ball, leaving the circular mark. I quickly photographed both marks, then borrowed the older farmer's claspknife and cut both patches of paint-covered hide out of the carcasses. I placed these in a small plastic bag I carry in my camera hold-all.

Instructing the truck driver to follow me to Guelph, I climbed into my wagon. Another late supper, I thought. The driver suddenly jumped out of his cab and ran up to me.

"Who's paying me for this?" he asked. "I can't work for nothing. I'm not like my brother, he's got a steady job."

I reassured him the Society would pay normal trucking charges. Again I prepared to drive away. This time the father trotted up from his throbbing tractor. "What about my time?" he shouted above the noisy diesel.

"Send me the bill," I shouted back. Finally I drove off, followed by the truck driver, now smiling, and a large attendant cloud of flies.

The technician at the receiving wing of the pathology department accepted the two bodies without comment, listing the tests I requested on the receiving form.

"Can I go then?" asked the truck driver.

"Yes, please," I replied. "The mileage was sixty-seven miles."

"Oh, you noted it then?"

"I certainly did."

"Can I have supper out?"

"At your expense, you can."

His face fell.

Two days later I received the results of the tests by phone, to be followed by the written report. "There's absolutely no blood in the carcass," reported the pathologist. "Just plasma. There was evidence of *Clostridae* bacteria in the soft organs. The genitalia were apparently surgically removed, as was the tongue. I really can't say what killed them. There are no wounds. Apart from the *Clostridae* both animals were in good health. The blood business is very puzzling."

I thanked the pathologist and hung up. I scanned the notes I had made during our telephone conversation. *Clostridae* harboured anthrax, but that had not killed two apparently healthy beasts. They seemed to have just fallen down devoid of red blood cells, and something, or someone, had cut off their tongues and sex organs. This was exactly the same as the recent cases in Alberta.

I took my paint-splashed scraps of hide downtown to

the Provincial Crime Laboratory, then I telephoned the RCMP in Alberta. The investigating officer was out, so while I awaited his reply I called the Cattlemen's Association and enquired if they were interested in offering a reward for information leading to the arrest and conviction of the persons responsible. They certainly were.

No other bodies of cattle were found. My friendly constable in Forest Hills had no leads. "The press have noticed it on our daily blotter. Will you talk to them?" he asked. I agreed I would.

Within the hour an earnest young woman reporter called me for comment.

"Frankly," I said, "we and the police are baffled by these mysterious deaths."

"Do you think it's devil worship?" she asked.

"No. I've got an open mind and an open telephone line. Anyone with useful information can call me collect." I mentioned the Stockmen's reward and added a further five hundred from the Society. The reporter said thanks and dashed off to make the bi-weekly edition on time. The article was placed front page centre.

The crime laboratory had given my paint scraps low priority. "Call us next week" was the reply to my request for information. In the interim I canvassed Humane Societies in the U.S.A. for information. There was nothing on record.

A lady who kept eighteen rabbits and a Shetland pony in her kitchen entered my schedule at this point. By the time I had sorted that out, the written pathology report had arrived. It cast no further light on the matter. I considered the case moodily. The phone rang.

"Will you accept a collect phone call from Forest Hills regarding the cattle," asked May.

"Will I!" I almost ran downstairs and hugged her. "Sure, put him on."

"Go ahead, sir. You're through to the chief inspector."

"Hulloo, hulloo, you the fellah with the reward?" asked a rough voice.

I agreed I was that person. Who was this, please?

"Name's Eli Pond. I live on the Asprey Township town line, 'bout three mile from where them beeves was. You recording this call?" he asked.

I assured him I was not.

"Well, I tell ya," Eli went on, "why doncha come round and see us? I think we got something."

I arranged to see him at his home that evening about six-thirty. Of course I missed supper again.

The town line road was a transportation no-man's-land. Neither community claimed it, and in consequence it went ungraded and unmended. The potholes reminded me of giant Pacific clams waiting to trap the unwary small cars. By a process of elimination I arrived in Eli Pond's driveway. Three husky-collie crossbred dogs exploded from under the insulbrick and tarpaper house as I stopped. A thin, unshaven man dressed in a dirty striped flannel shirt and grimy worn tweed trousers emerged from the house and shouted the dogs off.

I stayed in the car watching Eli approach. He had an ancient tweed cap on his head that appeared to have had a recent oil change, judging from the grease oozing from the sweatband. He had little brown eyes coupled with a sharp-pointed nose. He reminded me of an English Gypsy peg-maker I once knew.

"What about the reward, then?" he asked without ceremony, licking his thin lips.

"The reward is payable on the arrest and conviction of those responsible. What's your information?"

"Well it's like this," began Eli. I could sense the story would be a long one.

"Shall we walk round your barn?" I asked, wanting to put him at ease.

"Sure," he grunted.

I followed him to the dilapidated structure he fondly called his barn, picking my way between discarded car batteries, old tires, bits of motor vehicle and boxes of unidentifiable junk. When I caught up with Eli I asked him why he had not passed the information to the police. He gave me a pitying look.

"Couldn't, could I?"

"Why not?"

"We was doin' a bit of fishin', that's why. I hope you're gonna keep this between the two of us."

He proceeded to tell me that his cousin Irving and he, with another person he declined to name, had set out after dark one night to net out a pool on the Saugeen River. The river flowed through his property and that of a neighbour, the man who had lost the two steers. This sort of foray was a regular occurrence to Eli and his clan. They knew the ground intimately and could manage the nets, the water and the ground without need of anything other than a small flashlight. By about eleven o'clock the night was dark, since there was no moon, perfect for the poaching expedition. There was no afterglow from towns, buildings or installations.

Eli and company were just about to pull their net together and run it up the bank when, without warning or lights, over the trees whirred a helicopter. As one man Eli and company thought, "Game wardens!" Cousin Irving and the other man dropped the net and ran off downstream, everyone getting drenched in the process. Eli didn't run. He lay wet and dripping under a bush. His companions splashed away, but woods-wise and wily Eli, like Brer Rabbit, just lay low and didn't say nothing. He just watched. He noted that the hovering aircraft directed a beam of intermittent and fragmented light down to the ground from its underside. The beam was directed at a steer, and after two short false starts a longer burst of light was emitted. The steer fell down. "Just fell on its nose and rolled over. Funny thing, though, when the light was on, my ears hurt."

Following this, the steer remained still. Then the same thing happened again and another steer crashed to the ground. The helicopter hovered even lower, six or eight feet above the ground. Three men descended from a ladder lowered from the belly of the machine. They walked around the dead cattle for some minutes, then returned carrying a basket between them. The basket was handed up. The men climbed the ladder, which was then retracted. And all the while, quaking, shivering, Eli lay wet and wondering under the bushes.

Twice the beam had been directed at the cattle. Twice a steer had crashed on its nose. Eli couldn't comprehend what he had seen.

"What colour was the helicopter?" I asked.

"It was dark, almost black."

"What type?"

"I dunno. It had one rotor on top and was thick and deep in the body, with a funny thing sticking out of the top."

"I don't suppose you happened to see a number on it anywhere?"

"You're joking. I couldn't have seen one even if it was there." He looked up. "Well, what do you think it's worth?"

I concluded the notes I had been taking and put my notebook away. "I don't know what it's worth, but if it proves positive you'll get your reward."

The aircraft described by Eli, I realized, must be of a military nature or highly illegal. Surely, I mused as I drove home, the air-traffic control people would know of such an aircraft.

They did and they didn't. Asking for information was one thing. Getting it was another. The senior controller on duty agreed an aircraft had been conducting "flight tests" in the area, but as it was operating at less than two thousand feet, it was not on any approach pattern and operated independently. At this point the manager of the control centre came on the line to say that, as the aircraft was of a military nature, it had been routed through Downsview military control and no other details were available. So it *was* military.

Next question: Canadian or American? But another

country operating illegally in Canada? Could it really happen? I drove to the Downsview military base and asked to see the chief operations officer. After ten minutes of voices arguing in an adjoining office, he emerged. He proved to be a major, dark and dapper and of Quebec parentage. Frankly he wasn't interested in discussing the matter with any civilian, much less a genuine Englishman. Out of sheer curiosity I asked him the name of his home town. He looked at me as if such things were beyond my ken. But he told me, Maniwaki.

Reaching into my memory I mentioned everyone in Maniwaki I could remember: Hans Anderson, Clifford Gagne, Mr. Poirierre . . .

"Oh, so you know Maniwaki," my major said with surprise and delight. Most people he had met had never even heard of the place, let alone been there. Here, to his amazement, was an Englishman who not only had been there but had friends amongst the residents. After this warming trend, he said, "In reply to your question, all I can say is that the aircraft was engaged in night evaluation tests."

"What's that supposed to mean?" I asked.

"My friend, it means they were testing equipment and I don't have any more information."

"Did they use hangar facilities here?"

My major looked at his notes. "No. Elsewhere." He looked up and shrugged. I thanked him sincerely and left. I thanked heaven for past summers spent fishing on Lake Baskatong. But where the hell had my phantom helicopter gone?

Driving home along Keele Street, I turned over in my mind the information I now had. If it wasn't serviced at Downsview, where was the helicopter serviced? It must have been at a military base. And the nearest one was Quinte.

It just happened that I had had a complaint about the birds of prey runway clearance service at, of all places, Quinte. It seemed clear to me that now was the time to investigate that small complaint I hadn't had time for previously.

Next day found me in my Eagle wagon hammering east down the 401 to Quinte. It was raining and the clouds were low. These were, as they say, poor flying conditions. If there were any interesting aircraft on the ground, this was a good day to find them. I turned off the 401, alongside the Trent River, and rolled into the air base minutes later.

I stopped at the guardhouse and asked for the birdman, John Roofer.

"Please wait over there, sir," grunted the military policeman on duty at the gate. "We will radio Mr. Roofer to meet you here."

I sat in my wagon and looked out across the base. The wet, bare runways were inhabited by several score of gulls. No doubt there was a bird problem and it didn't seem so small after all. Then I saw a small Japanese truck moving along the service road adjacent to the runway. It had two speakers mounted on the roof. When the truck neared a flock of gulls, it slowed down and the speakers emitted the high-pitched *squawk* of a gull in distress. In unison the hundred or so gulls in that particular flock erupted in flight.

John Roofer drove over to me. He greeted me warmly and opened the rear of his vehicle to show me the falcons he employed when the tape recording proved ineffective. There, sitting on separate perches, wearing tasseled leather hoods, sat a Saker falcon and a Langar falcon. Both species were outside the scope of the Migratory Game Birds Act. But, I thought, having them might be an offence under the Endangered Species Act if he has no permit. Almost as if he had read my thoughts, John pointed to a photocopy of his permit taped to a sunvisor in his cab.

Listening to John Roofer is a real treat for anyone who enjoys birds. He has a great concern for all birds, not just his own. We sat and talked. I asked to enter the base with him in order to watch him work. He agreed, but the military police were not so enthusiastic. It took fifteen minutes of arguing and hard telephoning before I was issued a visitor's permit and sternly warned to stay in Mr. Roofer's vehicle. I smiled politely and agreed. John drove onto the base before anyone could have a change of mind.

Several aircraft sat outside on dispersal alert and perhaps many more in the open hangars. All had the silvery gleam of service aircraft. A white-painted Comet, a visitor from the Royal Air Force, was the sole visible exception. To the north of the field stood other buildings, some surrounded by large grass-covered banks and an additional fence. From my own service days, I knew these to be the explosives and ammunition stores. Further along this row stood a large Butler-type building, also inside a separate fence. I prevailed upon John to drive past this building and park.

He squawked the loudspeaker several times to scare off one small flock of gulls who looked as though they might become permanent residents on the grass strip. We sat for several minutes as the gulls circled, then John subjected the gulls to a two-second blitz of screeching. Wonder of wonders, a door in the Butler building opened and a man came out. He was tall and well tanned, with the short haircut of servicemen the world over. He wore a blue windbreaker, beige-coloured trousers and brown hunting boots.

"What's happened?" he asked.

Seizing the opportunity, I got out and ran over to him. "Sorry to bother you. My friend is demonstrating his bird scarer for me."

"Is that what it is? Jeeze, I thought someone's undercarriage had locked."

He had a distinct southern drawl. "You're not from around here," I said.

He smiled. "No, guess not."

"You're an American," I continued.

"Yeah, guess I am."

"You from Texas?" I asked.

He looked surprised. "Yeah, how'd you know?"

"Oh, I just guessed."

"Pretty good guesser for an Englishman."

"Yes, aren't I," I said modestly. "What's your home town?"

"Lubbock," he replied.

"Isn't that where Mac Davis is from? He said heaven was Lubbock, Texas—in his rearview mirror. Do you feel that way about it?"

He smiled again. "No, it's not that bad. Ever been there?"

"No, I went to Galveston, Corpus Christi, Padre Island, and up the Rio Grande Valley back to San Antonio and Houston. Very impressive. I expected to see Rock Hudson or Liz Taylor come riding out of one of those ranch gates any minute. Didn't though." He laughed and I continued. "So what brings you to this rainy place?" I asked, all innocence.

"The U.S. Army," he said with a slight hesitation. "Flight studies. I drew guard duty today. That's why I'm here and not in the barracks."

"Not much of a day for flying, is it?"

"No, it's not, but it's no matter to us, we work nights. Testing night-flying equipment."

"Really," I said. "That must be nerve-wracking."

He eyed me a little coldly. "Sometimes it is. Well, I'd best be getting indoors. It's wet out here."

"Yes, bye now."

I turned to go but turned back to watch him open the building's door. As he did so I saw the aircraft for testing night-flying equipment. It was a helicopter and it was painted a dark midnight-blue. The Konica didn't fail me in the wet. When I later developed the 400 ASA Kodak film, it showed the distinct outline of the craft. But no distinguishing mark or letters showed on the print. That was because there were none.

"Ever been here when that aircraft goes out, John?" I asked.

"No, and I've never been here when it comes back either," he replied. "Fancy some lunch?"

"Sure, where are we eating?"

"Over at the mess hall. You get a real good meal there for a dollar."

I returned my camera to its waterproof case.

Spooning applesauce on the pork chops I'd chosen at the buffet-style meal the armed forces offered its servicemen and civilian employees, I sat down with John and took a long drink of my cold milk. As I did so I took a long look at the men and women in the hall. Over in a corner were five more men dressed in a fashion similar to that of the American serviceman I had spoken to. They sat apart, conversing amongst themselves.

After lunch John was all set to bid me farewell. He wanted to fly the younger of the falcons and strangers made her nervous, or so he said.

"O.K., so you want to get rid of me. Tell you what, before I go let's check the birds at the garbage dump. I'd be interested to see what you do about controlling them."

"I don't," he replied. "It's not in my contract. But come to mention it, I should check it just to see the wet garbage is bulldozed in, so as to stop their feeding on it."

We drove to a secluded part of the base, behind a screen of trees. The place smelled of rot, garbage and spoiled food. It was infested with gulls and crows, fighting amongst themselves for the more choice pieces of smelly waste.

John played his screamer while I walked along the edge of the trench where the garbage, packed in green garbage bags, was stacked. A group of several gulls were fighting over something they had pecked out of a burst bag. They even resisted the screamer.

This must be good, I thought to myself when they almost resisted me as I walked over to them. I turned over the slimy scrap they were fighting for. It was the pecked remains of what could have been an ox tongue.

John drove over to me in his truck. "Come on, Don, this place is putting me off lunch."

"Sure," I said. "Tell you what, let's go back to the mess hall. I'd like an apple to take the taste of this place away."

We returned to the now almost empty mess hall. I picked up two apples for thirty cents from the catering staff.

"Tell me," I asked the corporal caterer in charge, "when do you fellows serve cold tongue in jelly? I love it."

The N.C.O. looked at me a little strangely. "We don't, some of these guys would throw it at us if we did. Anyway," he went on, "all our meat comes in primary cuts. We don't even get offal like liver unless we order it special."

I munched on one of my apples. "Thanks a lot, anyway," I said.

After saying thanks and farewell to John Roofer, I drove back to the office in the rain. Despite its being in a tightly tied plastic bag—one of those I always carry in my camera case—the gull-scrabbled tongue smelled foul. It smelled even after I washed it in a mixture of Javex, lavatory cleaner and cold water.

I put on my reading glasses and got out my Sherlock Holmes magnifying glass. There was no stamp in either the red or blue ink used by meat inspectors to show inspected slaughter in a provincial or federal packing plant, as required by law for animals slaughtered for human consumption. Meat from animals not for human consumption is stained green. There was nothing at all on this one, therefore it had come from an illegal slaughter. A farm slaughter could also be ruled out, for no farmer would throw away a whole tongue. I stored the tongue in two fresh bags and an exhibit box tightly sealed, and popped it into the freezer in the office refrigerator.

On my way home I stopped at the public library, where I located a copy of Jane's *World's Aircraft*. I spent my military service in the army, so aircraft are foreign to me. However, I soon came upon the helicopter I had glimpsed in the hangar. There it was, a "Bell model 206L, the Texas Ranger . . . carries up to eight persons, including a crew of two . . . has a TOW gunsight on roof." (That would be the "funny" thing Eli spoke of.) ". . . has infra-red camera and established infra-red binoculars."

How come they missed seeing Eli? I asked myself, and had the answer. Eli was wet, cold, soaking. The infra-red camera works on heat. Eli, in hiding under the tree, had escaped detection because of the soaking he'd experienced. I drove home very thoughtfully indeed to salad, cold meat and pickles.

"What would you prefer to do," I asked the director. "The evidence is purely circumstantial. It won't stand up in court, even if we got them there."

"Oh, come on, Don, we can't arrest visiting Americans on a twopenny-ha'penny thing like this."

"With all respect, it's not a twopenny-ha'penny thing," I said. "Killing cattle is a felony, an indictable offence, punishable by five years in Her Majesty's vile jail. Section 400 of the Criminal Code is quite specific on that point. Speaking for myself, I suggest that perhaps we could lay the fact before the M.P. for the district and get him to ask questions in the House. That would bring things into the open and perhaps scare them off."

"That's an excellent idea," said the director. "I'll set it up for you."

True to his word, the director had the appointment set up at the Honourable Member's riding office. Before meeting him, however, I was required to set out the facts in memorandum form. The whole thing read like something out of the *Boy's Own Paper* or the *Hotspur*.

I remembered reading in a magazine article that cattle had been found dead and mutilated in Wyoming. I dialled the Stockmen's Association there. When the representative came on the line, I asked him if any of his members had experienced any cattle mutilations. They certainly had. So had their neighbours in Nebraska. The Nebraska Stockmen's Association also confirmed losing cattle, and mentioned similar instances in Iowa and that they had employed a private detective from Maryland who had made many enquiries.

Calling the private detective was easy. Getting him to reply was another story. But reply he did—at eleven-thirty that night. What he said was amazing. He had been retained by two stockmen's associations in neighbouring states to look into the cattle mutilations. What he had discovered was that, in all, one thousand five hundred head had been found dead and mutilated in twenty-two states. He also confirmed the blue paint on the shoulders. But what really staggered me was when he said, "They kill them with some sort of ultrasonic ray gun. It breaks down the red corpuscles and reduces the blood to a watery plasma."

"Have you any idea where it's originating from?" He confessed himself baffled. What he did say was that the mutilations had *not* occurred in California, Arizona, Oregon, Washington, New Mexico, Texas or the southeastern U.S., including Florida. Utah and Idaho had experienced very few. I thanked him and gave him what scant information I had, but did not mention the helicopter or my witness.

Making myself a pot of tea in the kitchen, I sat down with a map of the United States and drew a pencil line north to south on the western borders of New Mexico and Colorado, continuing through the western third of Wyoming, then angling it slightly west to include Calgary. I then drew a line east to west, using as my base line the southern border of Kansas. The area north and east of the angle of those two lines had suffered most of the mutilations. Sipping my tea, I speculated that if all these cattle had *Clostridae* bacteria, they could have been infected by the prevailing wind carrying the spores by way of the jet stream. The point of origin in that case would be in Colorado.

Next day I went back to the public library. Dipping into a volume on the United States Defence estimates for the past year, I came upon the fact that chemical and bacterial warfare research had been, or was presently being, studied at Fort Dix, New Jersey, Fort Dietrich, Maryland, Pine Bluff, Arkansas, and the Dugway Proving Grounds, Utah. But what really jumped out and hit me was the plainly printed information that all the agents for the above experiments were stored at the Rocky Mountain Arsenal. In *Colorado*.

Just supposing you wanted to test out a bacterial agent, wanted to release some infinitesimal percentage of what you would use in a real war situation, say 0.0001 percent. How would you disperse it high enough to catch the jet stream? A rocket? Too obvious. Aircraft? Perhaps, but what type? Once again I went back to Jane's. "The U2 Lockheed TR-1A (the Blackbird) . . . still in use, has a wing span of one hundred feet, speed of four hundred and thirty miles an hour and a ceiling of 90,000 feet." There, it would seem, was a method of launch. I handed in the books and went back to my office. There I sat still, just thinking for a long time.

During my initial enquiries, Mr. Tasman, the owner of the dead steers, had casually mentioned that he had bought the steers at a calf auction in Pincher Creek, Alberta. Had someone in the U.S. military caused the death and mutilation of cattle in Alberta and south of the border? Had they tracked the group of calves all the way to Asprey Township, Ontario, just to slaughter two samples to test their theory of germ warfare?

Two days later I received the summons to the M.P.'s riding office. We arrived shortly before six o'clock, the time appointed to meet the Honourable Member.

"Do come in and sit down, gentlemen," said his secretary.

"Glad to meet you fellows," said the M.P. from behind his desk.

The director introduced me.

"This is Mr. Guine from National Defence," said the M.P., motioning to a tall grey-haired man with gold-rimmed spectacles.

Again we shook hands all round.

"Oh, here's your report. Good. Here's a copy for you, Fern." He handed the man from Ottawa a copy.

They both read my memorandum through twice, put it down and stared at me, hard.

"Where are things now, then?" asked the M.P.

I brought them up to date, adding my speculation about the method of distribution and origin.

"How many persons know of this?"

"No one but the four of us knows the complete story, so far as I'm aware," I answered.

Mr. Guine looked at me. "What about your wife?" he asked.

"I don't tell her all my business and I don't ask her all hers," I replied.

Mr. Guine smiled. "An amiable arrangement, my friend."

"Well, of course," said the M.P., "I'll certainly ask the Minister in the House. I'll have to ask him for compensation for the farmer—and for you fellows, of course." He studied me for some seconds through narrowed eyes. "I do congratulate you, sir," he said to the director, "on having such a perceptive and diligent investigator. You certainly know how to find the right man for the job."

"Yes," agreed the director, "I think I know how to pick the men with the right stuff."

"Well, I won't keep you. You've a long drive back. My office will be in touch. Bye." We were dismissed.

Two weeks later, on the television program that recounts the day in Parliament, I watched to see our M.P. rise to his feet to ask the Minister the question. No such mention. Instead we received an extract from Hansard:

"The Minister of Defence, in a written reply to the Right Honourable Member's Question, stated that 'it is not at present expedient to reveal the military activities referred to at present. It would not be in the public interest'."

Feeling crushed, I went off for a light lunch and spent the rest of the afternoon in a very smelly barn that proudly advertised itself as a breeding kennel. Returning to the office at four-thirty, I found the director in. Occasionally he returns about four-thirty. He wants to see if anyone has sneaked off early. Today he was in one of his more expansive moods.

"Ah, Donald, lad. Come in and sit down. I've had news from the Minister. Very good news. Thanks to your efforts we shall be receiving a very nice cheque, very nice indeed."

"Ah, does that mean a small raise, then?" I asked brightly. I'm not bashful when the time is opportune.

"Well, I don't see why you shouldn't have another thousand a year, eh what. Must reward hard work and enterprise."

Mmmm, that worked out to nineteen dollars a week, nearly the price of a bottle of painkiller. "Thanks very much, Sir, very good of you."

"Not at all, Don, you're first-class at this job."

"EEEEEeeeeeeeek!" There was a scream from the staff common room. We all rushed there to find May, our receptionist, collapsed on the floor. The door to the small cupboard refrigerator hung open and there, on the turf-green carpet, in its plastic bag, but still managing to smell vile, was the maggot-infested steer tongue I'd popped in the cold compartment for safekeeping and forgotten all about.

Gulping down my own revulsion, I picked up the smelly object, took it outside, and dropped it in the garbage. I was just about to re-enter when I heard May's sorrowful voice, full of injury.

"Mr. Hepworth's always doing things like that, Sir! What about the time he brought all those horse legs here. It's too much. He shouldn't be allowed to bring nasty things like that to the office."

I had second thoughts about returning to the office. I

thought on the whole it would be a good idea if I went home and brushed my newest horse. I'd even be able to have my dinner on time. I hoped my wife hadn't prepared my once favourite dish—though not served at Canadian Air Force bases. I refer, of course, to boiled tongue.

THE LAKELAND DOG MASSACRE

MEDONTE IS A QUIET TOWN. IT'S FAIRLY QUIET AS FAR as animals go, too, until autumn, when the hunting season arrives, then it becomes the central collecting point for hounds, beagles and hunting dogs of all breeds and shapes.

The woods north of Medonte are hard hunted, not only by residents of Ontario, but by citizens of the U.S.A., from as far afield as Ohio and New Jersey. Hunters flock into the woods, release their hounds and hope they return. Frequently, they do not. Poorly trained dogs run themselves into exhaustion after three days. Starving and spent, they are found on concession roads and picked up by the Humane Society's drivers. Many are then claimed from us, usually by local owners, but an equal number are never claimed. Ultimately, they have to be destroyed.

It was with thoughts of these hunting dogs that I listened to a story told by Winifred, one of our supervisors. She had telephoned me early in the afternoon, her voice showing concern. A heap of dead dogs had been found on a back road near Lakeland. The dogs had been covered by snow all winter, but now they had been discovered.

By leaving home at six the following morning, I arrived at the site of the dog carcasses just after eight-thirty. Thankfully, it had been a cold spring night and there was no noticeable smell from the bodies of the twenty-odd dead canines.

I stood for some moments just looking at the two low piles of bodies. Snow covered them partially and I photographed the scene from several different angles. The Bell telephone line crew drove up. It had been they who had telephoned the Society the day before. Their supervisor approached me while the workers began to put out plastic traffic cones outlining their work area.

"We found this lot yesterday," he said by way of introduction. "Weird scene, isn't it?"

Nodding absently, I agreed with him. It was obvious I would discover little at the site itself, so with the two agents from Medonte who had joined me there, I set about loading the pathetic dead animals into a hired box truck. None, I noticed, had collars or tags.

We laid the bodies out in two lines of ten and eleven on the concrete yard of the Medonte shelter and hosed them down with cold water. It was clear the animals had not died violently. There were no wounds visible. Another notable fact was the evidence of age among the dead animals. Most of the dogs showed the grey muzzles of aging. An agent and I photographed the group again.

Later I pulled on my coveralls, rubber boots and gloves. Armed with forceps, tweezers and a powerful hand lamp, I set about a careful examination of every body. After an hour and a half of smelly, disgusting work, I had two clues. On two dogs I had found shaven places on the front left forelegs, and in the ear of one Labrador retriever, I had noted a tattooed registration number that indicated connection with a registered breeder. Saving those three bodies in the deep freeze, we took the remainder to the Toronto area crematorium for disposal.

It took three weeks to trace the origin of the Labrador retriever. The tattoo mark had been issued to a breeder in London, Ontario, so the Kennel Club records said. I drove to London.

"Ah, that would be one of Mayblossom's litter in 1968," the breeder informed me. "She was a good bitch. We had to put her down last year. She developed fits, you know."

The breeder took me into her office. She pressed a whisky and soda on me as she thumbed through three fat record books.

"There it is!" she exclaimed, looking up after fifteen minutes of thumbing through well-worn papers. "I sold two bitches out of the same litter to Brian Fleet. He trains up near Kincardine."

Pausing only to thank her, I turned my wheels northwest and cooked a little rubber in the direction of Georgian Bay.

Brian Fleet trained dogs on evenings, Saturdays, Sundays and holidays. At other times he sold farm machinery. I arrived at his kennels at five-thirty that afternoon and found him mixing bowls of kibble and meat for the dogs' evening meal.

"Yes, I remember 'the twins,' as we called them. Still got one of the pair here." He gave a thin reedy whistle and the black Labrador bitch bounded up from the creek bed below us. She attempted to peer into his mouth. "This is Blossom," he said. "The other was called Daisy, and I sold her to a guy who does field trials."

"Do you have his name? Can you recall where he lives?" I asked.

"Now you have me," he replied, "but I can tell you one thing. He lived on the Lake of Bays, somewhere on the east shore. If I think of anything else, I'll give you a call."

I had to content myself with that for the time being.

I drove home in an ill humour. Next day I felt no better as I set out on the three-hour drive to the Lake of Bays. Fortunately, it was a fine day and spring was decidedly showing as I negotiated the switchback road that leads to Dwight. The willows were golden, and on the ground green fern tops were pushing through the dead brown foliage of last year. A pair of evening grosbeaks skittered across the road before me. The air smelled of a woody wine. I whistled Vaughn William's version of the Somerset folk tune "Seventeen Come Sunday" as I soared and dived along the county road.

"Black Labrador retriever," mused the owner of the village store when I asked her if she knew of one. "No, not really. You see, we can't encourage dogs in the shop. The males do spoil the apples so."

Reminding myself not to buy any apples there, I thanked her and went to the municipal offices.

The township clerk nodded understandingly when I explained my errand. "We just issue the tags in numerical order," he explained, "but we do record the breed on the licence."

I had a brief lunch, then set about flipping my way through the seven hundred and forty-two dog licences that had been issued by the township. An hour and a half later, I knew there were nine black Labrador dogs licensed.

The co-operative by-law officer allowed me to use his telephone in my continuing effort to locate the trainer and/or owner of the deceased black Labrador. I succeeded in narrowing the field down to two females, but there was no reply to calls made to the numbers listed for either licence. Thanking the by-law officer for the use of his phone and the hand-drawn district map that indicated the dog owners' properties, I set off along the winding wooded roads.

I arrived at the first owner's residence within half an hour. It was plain they had a dog on their property—I could hear one barking inside the wooden cottage—but it did not appear at the windows and there was no answer to my knocking. I walked slowly round the outside of the cottage. If I could see the black Labrador, I could move on to the next house. The drapes were drawn throughout the house except in one window, where there was a gap in the curtains high at the upper edge of the material. Standing on a soft-drink crate, I tried to look through the triangular space. As I did so, the curtains were pulled back quickly and a tearful boy of about seven screamed at me through the window, "Leave me alone, mister!" I was shocked, stepped back, missed my footing and fell flat on my backside. The boy continued to howl.

"Have you got a dog?" I yelled back when I had picked myself up.

"Yes," he sobbed, "it's a big, fierce dog. It bites! Please go away, mister!"

I was not in uniform. The lad looked at me again, really wild-eyed now. In his estimation, I was a burglar. The mother drove up in a small car. "Wayne's a disturbed kid," she said. "He's also off school with chicken pox this week and he hates being left alone all day. He imagines all sorts of things. I'm separated. Come in and I'll show you our dog. My husband bought her somewhere. I'll try to find her papers for you if you like."

Since the family had a live black Labrador, they had removed themselves from the list.

So the last person on the list was the person I needed to interview. The address was the inevitable rural route. I looked at the sun, now below treetop level, a brilliant red. "Red at night, sailors' delight," I thought to myself, "red in the morning, shaky day."

This must be the place, an insulbrick house with lights on inside. The man I needed to see would not be home, I bet myself. I was right.

"No, he's away logging," said the woman who answered the door. "They're taking out a section at Kiosk." Kiosk was the northern edge of Algonquin Park, miles away. "I'm sorry," the woman went on, "he's never had a dog since I met him. I think he used to have one, but not of late."

"Could I ask you how long you've known him?"

"Oh, since Christmas," she smiled. "Would you like to come in?"

"Not unless I can talk to him on the phone."

"Well, he phones me most every evening from a call box. He lives in his truck, you see."

Next day found me grinding along in low gear, trying to cope with the deep mud of a park logging road. By sheer good luck, I arrived at the centre dead on noon, when all hands were in for lunch. I found the late dog's owner downing a plate full of stew. He invited me to join him, which I did. We sat side by side spooning down stew and corn bread. Over a mug of coffee and a large chunk of apple pie, my witness told his tale.

"I had old Daisy seven years. Bought her from a guy up near Kincardine. Trained her myself, and she was good. Won a fair number of trophies with her. Retired her at six to breed her. One day she ran across the road and got hit by a car. She lay still for two days, then she got up and limped around. I took her to the vet, he gave me some pills for her. He said she'd be O.K., and she was for a while. Then she got arthritis and that got worse and worse. Finally she could hardly get around. I took her back to the vet. I paid him fifteen dollars to put her away with an injection and cremate her." He was silent.

So now I had it. The patches shaved for injection on the two bodies confirmed the story. I recorded the facts in a statement which my witness signed wordlessly. I thanked him and left.

Two days later, I stood in the veterinarian's office. I showed him the photographs, told him of my suspicions and cautioned him against making self-incriminating statements. He looked at me in disbelief for a moment, then shrugged his shoulders. He nodded and said, "Yes, I euthanized the dogs you found. I intended to get them cremated in Toronto, in the spring. I was keeping them in the garage at the beginning of winter, but my wife complained of the smell. So I put them in the woods during a snowstorm. Thought the wolves would take care of them, and the snow cover the remains."

My next stop was the Crown attorney. In my view the veterinarian had committed an offence against Section 319 of the Canadian Criminal Code. He had obtained money by false pretence. The Crown attorney did not agree with me at all. He flatly declined any action. So I complained to the Discipline and Ethics Committee of the Veterinarians' Association. The offending vet was reprimanded and fined six hundred dollars, which was twice the sum he had made destroying the twenty-one dogs at fifteen dollars each. It was a good deal more than a criminal court would have fined him, however.

He's still in practice, but we haven't encountered any more piles of bodies in the woods. No new pet crematorium has been built up north either.

Some years later I suggested that if we couldn't afford a crematorium for the northern region, we should at least create a landfill site that could be properly controlled as a burial ground for pets as well. The last I heard, nothing had come of my suggestion. Yet there are still *more* people, *more* breeders, *more* vets in that area today than there were at the time the events in this story took place. And in conversation up there that pretty wooded lane is now called "Dead Dog Road."

CIRCUS
CIRCUS

EVERY YEAR A NUMBER OF CIRCUS ACTS IN NORTH America are gathered together under the sponsorship of the Shriners and the circus is called the "Shrine Circus." Basically, it's an entertainment originated and administered by the Shriners and aimed at raising money for certain charities. There are a lot of young children in the world today leading comfortable lives free of disfigurement because of the burn units funded by the chapters, or temples, of the Shriners.

The performers at this year's circus had arrived on time, pitching their wagons in the hierarchy laid down many, many years ago in Europe. The more important the artist or performer, the closer to the big-top performers' entrance he may park his wagon. On this occasion the circus members had tended their livestock, put down their ring, rigged the animals' wagons, and were relaxing before the afternoon performance.

The Shriners' advance team had handled the publicity efficiently. A great many tickets had been sold. All that remained was for the Shriners' ticket-takers, popcorn vendors and ancillary staff to open the doors and welcome the happy and expectant public. Instead, they got Muriel Wooler and her Animal Comfort League.

Muriel was a wealthy, independent woman without a family. She doted on animals of any kind. Any animal not absolutely clean or otherwise in show condition—sitting on a soft cushion, so to speak—was, according to her precepts, being ill treated. She had made it her mission in life to advise the world of this.

She arrived at the quietly resting circus with twenty members of her league. They carried placards denouncing the immorality of making animals perform tricks, etc. One of the group had tipped off a TV camera crew and a couple of journalists, and the media was on hand to get the story. Muriel and her friends were ready both to give them one and to reap the ensuing publicity for their cause.

The performers' door to the auditorium stood open. Before anyone was aware of what was happening, the Animal Comfort League was inside. The building, which did duty in winter as the community hockey rink, was empty of animals except for Captain Eduardo Miles's forest-bred lions. This group of ten was accommodated in five travelling cages, two lions to a cage.

In any group of animals, one will be lowest in the pecking order, and among these lions the lowest was Henry, a neutered and maneless male. On a recent occasion Henry had been slow in moving up the entrance tunnel into the ring and Negus, an unneutered, maned male, had urged Henry to move on by nipping his tail. As a result, Henry had a sore tail. The trainer, Ted Miles, of Baraboo, Wisconsin, had bandaged the sore tail neatly, but Henry still looked like what he was, a lion with a big bandage on his tail. Ted (otherwise known as Fearless Captain Miles) had considered leaving Henry out of the act. In fact he had actually done so once, but Henry had roared, moped and bellowed throughout the entire performance. He had complained so much that the other lions had become edgy and difficult to cue onto their places. It was easier and safer for all concerned to dose Henry with penicillin, keep his bandage clean and leave him in the act.

Muriel and her ladies didn't know this, of course, or even try to find out. They reacted with predictable indignation, demanding to know who was in charge of the lions. The few Shriners in the auditorium clearly were not lion trainers. The chief Shriner told them so. He also told them to leave.

"Not until we get help for this poor lion," Muriel shouted.

The police were sent for. Hearing this, the Animal Comfort League slowly retreated outside among the trailers and beast wagons. There they encountered Mario and his Gypsy Bears.

Mario Blavitch had originally seen gypsies with bears in his native Yugoslavia. This had been before his immigration to the United States, where he had hoped to continue his trade as plumber. Unfortunately, his knowledge of the English language was insufficient to pass the U.S. Trade Test for a plumber, and by some series of accidents he had become a bear trainer instead. It was his habit before the show to exercise Nikky, his large male bear, by trotting him up and down the lot. He and Nikky trotted into the Animal Comfort League's rather scattered ranks just as the members were working themselves up to full cry.

"Let this poor abused animal go!" demanded Muriel of the bear trainer.

"Pliss, no understand," replied Mario, thoroughly confused and unable to read the league's placards.

The noise brought out the other performers, who were no strangers to demonstrations of this type, and they wasted no time in advising the league. In fact the performers told them exactly where to go in language that surmounts all international boundaries.

The league soon rallied. They followed Mario to the beast van, where he urged Nikky back into his cage. There they saw Pappy, a male Galaga baboon that Mario had helped to train. Its act was to walk along with a small bear, imitating Mario himself. On seeing Pappy they took up a new cry: "Poor monkey!" Some of the more militant began hitting Mario with their placards. But by now Mario had had enough. He reached under the van to the wheelbarrow full of fresh droppings. Turning, he pelted the ladies with handfuls of baboon and bear droppings. They retreated.

Meanwhile the reporters and newsreel camera crew had not been idle. Scenting news, they had been following along behind the group. Now they walked up to Mario. He pelted them with manure, too. A reporter, microphone in hand, tried to approach Mario in an effort to get a word or two from him. Mario repeated his two international words of departure, following them up with more manure. The news crew also retreated under fire.

The police arrived, took a few names and addresses, and stood by to prevent further breaches of the peace. A highly edited version of the day's events appeared on the evening television news and the Humane Society received a monumental complaint from Muriel, who was as eloquent on the telephone as in person.

Looking at the circus's schedule, I saw that the next performance was due the following afternoon some twenty miles away. I called Stu to assist me and he duly arrived an hour before the performance. Muriel and company were there, picketing the front of the arena. We drove round the back to the animal wagon park. The policemen detailed to keep Muriel's league away from the animals let us through.

Mario was already running Nikky up and down, warming him up for the performance. Madame Clara was preparing her three elephants.

Tied to the fence bordering the parking lot, Harrison's Amazing Mules were eyeing us. These were six albino mules that looked rather like large white mice, with their tall ears and harmless gaze. However, as we were to learn soon enough, they were cunning, mischievous and accomplished escapists. We walked past them to look at the lions. We had come to see Henry.

Henry was sitting in the last of the five cages. He wore a khaki-coloured bandage round his tail and a dazed expression on his face. His cage mate, an unneutered, maned male, watched us suspiciously with his ears flattened. Fearless Captain Miles came up as we arrived.

"Good afternoon, Captain. Which vet is attending this lion?" I asked.

"None," he answered. "I've never met a vet who knows a damned thing about big cats."

"Well, how long has this condition existed?"

"Ever since Tonawanda, three weeks ago. Look, it's better than it was."

"O.K.," I said, "but will you let a vet examine him if I get you one?"

"Oh, sure, but not now," he agreed cheerfully.

We said that we would come back with the vet the next morning. We then checked the bears and Pappy the baboon. They were clean and well nourished. Their travelling cages were, of necessity, small, but the animals were run out at least twice daily, so their muscles were kept fit.

The mules were all tied neatly to their fence. Their hooves were trimmed and oiled, their coats brushed, their tails combed out. Their hay nets were full for the animals to pick at, pending grain after the performance. The three elephants stood slowly swaying in the manner that elephants have. Madame Clara was enjoying a cigarette and a drink of some amber-coloured fluid in a small glass. She was well over sixty years of age, but her figure and legs, in her somewhat revealing costume and dark tights, were still good.

We thought we might as well eat, since there was nothing for us to attend to until performance time. The food outlet was also operated by the Shriners. The menu offered two items, fried chicken and chili. Stu had a generous portion of fried chicken. I had the chili. Looking for a quiet place to sit and eat, we were directed to the upper floor, where we found ourselves in the lobby of a theatre. We sat on one of the chesterfields that stood haphazardly against the walls.

The theatre itself was occupied by a meeting of the Sons of the Tartan. This is a fraternal organization open to males over twenty-one years of age who are of Caledonian parentage. As we sat eating, we watched the members arrive. Each brought a short kilt, which he donned in the Gents. Then he demanded admittance by knocking several times on the theatre door. A doorkeeper opened the door about six inches and demanded the password, holding up a claymore sword as he did so.

We watched several members arrive, dress and enter in this way. Some had more impressive accessories than others. One or two wore plaids and bonnets with eagle feathers, and cairngorm-jewelled pins. Some of the regalia represented considerable expense. From the conversation, we gathered that the Sons of the Tartan shared the meeting hall with the Knights of St. Pythias. This was confirmed about twenty minutes after the Sons had commenced their meeting.

As we sat sipping our coffee, a grand figure ascended the stairs. He was wearing evening dress with a tailed coat and white tie. He had an evening cape, top hat and a thin dress sword. We watched open-mouthed as this elegant fellow climbed the stairs and crossed the lobby. He halted at the door, the slender sword raised over his shoulder. He then knocked with the sword hilt five or six times on the door frame. Nothing happened. He repeated the business. The door opened a crack and a beady eye fixed him in its stare. "What's the password?" The fellow mumbled something. "Like hell it is," the doorkeeper replied. The door closed, then opened again. The doorkeeper, carrying his claymore, and a clan chieftain, holding an even bigger sword, confronted the intruder. The knight, it appeared, had arrived on the wrong night. Blushing with confusion, he apologized and left.

The chieftain turned to the doorkeeper. "Good job you're here. We wouldn't have wanted him inside. You didn't tell him the password, did you?"

"No, no fear. But I got his!"

The chieftain nodded at us. He went back inside and then returned with six of his clan, all of them carrying swords. "Where do you lads want to change?" he asked us.

Stu and I exchanged looks. "Change?" I said. "We're dressed for the job."

"Are you two not candidates for initiation?"

"No, we're Humane Society inspectors having ten minutes away from the animals."

"Damn it," he said, "only been Junior Chieftain two weeks and everything goes wrong. I'll be glad to be out of this chair."

Performance time had arrived, so we went down to watch the Grand Parade. Mario and his Gypsy Bears came first. The bears wobbled along on their hind legs, poker-faced, front paws hanging. The jugglers, acrobats, and trapeze artistes followed, waving to everyone. The white mule troop appeared. The elephants came last.

The circus proper then commenced, the forest-bred lions being the first act. We watched the adequate but not outstanding performance. You can't beat or whip a lion into doing anything it doesn't want to do. They willingly jump from stand to stand, in their own pecking order. The crack of the whip simply cues them when to go. But just tapping a show lion on the nose can produce a small charge or roaring match. It never fails to impress.

As the applause died, we watched the lions exit up their tunnel to their cages. Henry was first and he was a slowpoke, to be sure. He seemed reluctant to leave the applause. It was easy to see how he had come to be bitten. One of the attendants held an electric cattle prod. Normally, the animals would need no urging to leave the big arena cage—though they might need urging in. Among this group of big cats Henry appeared an exception. In this case the prod was on hand to break up any squabble, like the one that had resulted in Henry's bandaged tail.

As we watched the lions settle into their respective cages, each with its proper partner, a Shriner I recognized as a senior government veterinarian came in quickly and out of breath. "You chaps are needed out here, quick!"

We followed him outside, where we found Muriel and her Animal Comfort League. They had bypassed the solitary constable and were once again harassing the performers and animals. While the league members had been shouting at Mario—from a safe distance—the white mules had been quietly slipping their halters. Now the members imprudent enough to get close to the mules were being kicked anywhere and everywhere. Two of the mules frolicked among the elephants, kicking at them briskly.

It was too much for Annabel, Bebe and Cleo. Trunks up, ears out, tails stiffened behind them, they took off at their lumbering trot down the alley. Madame Clara tried valiantly to stop Cleo. The elephants were moving too fast, however, and the mules constantly obstructed her efforts.

Stu ran to our wagon and reached under the seat, coming up with a "bull hook." Holding the hook in his teeth, he jumped on a pedal cycle propped against a trailer and wobbled off behind the elephants, mules and Madame Clara. Grabbing my trusty stock cane, I sprinted along behind.

Stu rapidly overtook Madame Clara as the elephants lumbered along in the direction of the town's main intersection. A motorcyclist travelling in their wake stopped and offered me a ride. Gratefully, I hopped onto the pillion of his machine. As we drew close I was in time to see Stu hook Annabel in her left ear.

He was dragged off the bike. "Whoa!" he shouted. "Steady!" Annabel slowed. "Whoa!" he yelled again, and all three slowed. "Tails!" he commanded. Obediently, Bebe and Cleo each grasped the tails before them with their respective trunks.

The elephants were now in an orderly convoy, but still travelling in the direction of the main street. I jumped off the motorbike. "Stop here, please," I shouted. "We have to stop the traffic." A bus slowed, then stopped in line with the motorcyclist.

"Try and turn them, Stu," I yelled.

Stu nodded emphatically and sweat flew from the end of

his nose. "Come over!" he commanded. And praise be, Annabel answered to his voice and the pressure in her ear. She was turning left, the others following. Stu now had them walking back in the direction of the arena. I managed to catch one of the runaway mules. The others followed behind me.

The police had by now obtained reinforcements and stopped the traffic so that we could cross back up the alley. Madame Clara had caught up with us and she took charge of Bebe and Cleo. Stu walked the elephants up to their chains and secured them. I handed over my mule and assisted in collecting the other mischief-makers.

"Do you want to come work for me?" Madame Clara asked Stu.

He smiled shyly and said, "No, my wife wouldn't travel with a show."

"Well, anytime you change your mind."

The rest of the performance passed without incident. We were grateful for this, since our shirts were soaked with sweat from exertion and nerves. Muriel and her league were no longer in evidence. We left as "O Canada" ended and the hum of after-show voices began.

Next morning, after breakfast, we returned, in clean shirts, with a vet. The lion tamer showed up, surprised we had arrived on time. Again we went to Henry's cage, which he shared with his partner.

"We can't tranquillize the one without the other," said the vet.

We loaded two syringes with the required drug, clipping them in the end of the "push pole." In short order both lions were sleeping. The vet unwrapped Henry's tail bandage. A faint fuzz of tawny hair was growing through the pink area of healed skin. The animal was not in any pain or distress. There was absolutely no evidence of any neglect at all. Even so, we'd been called upon to investigate. And if we hadn't felt called upon as part of our job to check on Henry's tail injury, we wouldn't have been there having fun.

The circus moved on that morning. We waved them off.

"Drop in anytime," they called to us. "Come and work the pigs, Stu!" (Elephants are "pigs" in the circus.)

We smiled and shook our heads. There is no danger of Stu or me running away to join a circus. We are too fond of regular hot baths and clean shirts.

LITTLE
DOG
LOST

I DON'T USUALLY LISTEN TO ANIMAL SHELTER RADIO transmissions, since I'm out of radio range most of the time. However, on this particular day I was cruising east along the 401, coming back to Toronto from Guelph, where I'd been to a hearing to set a trial date for a citizen of that city. He'd been charged with leaving two hounds to starve while away in Florida hunting.

Listening to the radio I learned a Doberman pinscher was loose on the live runway at Toronto International Airport. While I didn't think a Doberman would be able to bite through aircraft tires, I thought it might intimidate a crew of baggage handlers on the tarmac. Two wardens were on their way to collect the stray Dobe when a cancellation request came over the air from the control tower: "No longer required." The wardens acknowledged and went off elsewhere. I concentrated on steering my way through the traffic and construction on the 401.

Arriving at the office I was greeted with the information that a crying lady wished to speak to me on the phone. I used the lobby desk to take the call. The lady caller was sobbing deeply, but after a little reassurance she composed herself enough to tell me her complaint.

It seemed she had returned from a three-month visit to her married daughter in Vancouver. Her dog, a Doberman pinscher, had accompanied her and the visit had been a good one. She had returned via Red and White Airlines and the Doberman had been obliged to travel in the freight hold in a travelling cage. All had been well until the freight was off-loaded on arrival at Toronto International Airport. By some truly amazing feat of mishandling, the cage had been overturned, the door had opened and the Doberman had run away—confused, frightened, lost.

For an hour or more her dog had run from loading bay to loading bay, listening for a familiar voice, while the one person who could have helped had been required to sit in the freight office "pending the solution," as the airline personnel put it, of "a slight technicality" with the freight. While she had sat there helplessly, her dog had tired of vehicle smells and the poor creature had made off for open country, crossing the live runway in its flight.

Fearing collision with a small plane scheduled to land at any moment, an RCMP officer had shot her dog with a high-powered rifle. She was asking us for help and advice.

I advised her to retain a competent lawyer and see an airline legal representative, as well as the commissioner of the RCMP. I also promised her that some enquiries would be made by us.

I drove out to the RCMP offices at the airport and asked for the officer who had shot the dog. After some evasion the senior officer on duty showed up. He said the officer in question had felt it was his duty to kill the dog to protect the pilot and passengers of the landing plane. I asked for a copy of their standing order on such a matter. It turned out there was none. The officer had acted on his own initiative.

I pointed out that the officer had contravened Section 401 of the Criminal Code by killing, without excuse, an animal that was kept for a lawful purpose. The senior officer looked at me with some alarm. I told him I'd consult the owner about laying the charge, and walked out.

The owner was under sedation for the rest of the day. Next morning we spoke again. I told her of my findings. She was still tearful. Her lawyer was in the process of preparing a monumental lawsuit against Red and White Airlines and the RCMP. No, she told me, she did not wish to attend court twice. Once would be quite enough. She was expecting twenty thousand dollars compensation and a public apology. She did finally succeed in being awarded some of the former but no apology was ever heard.

For the next few weeks my mind was occupied with slaughter horses in transit from Michigan to Charlemagne, Montreal. Dogs in the tender care of Red and White Airlines were far from my mind.

Then one evening I received a call, via our answering service, from Calgary of all places. I returned the call. The person I was calling was a Mr. Tcacs, a Canadian-Hungarian and a breeder of Hungarian kuvasz dogs. He told me, with tears in his voice, that he had recently shipped the best kuvasz bitch in North America to a buyer in Cleveland, Ohio. It had been necessary to ship by air via Toronto. The carrier, as I had already guessed, was Red and White Airlines. They had lost the dog.

According to his story, a PR woman from Red and White had telephoned Mr. Tcacs and, in a most conciliatory fashion, apologized for "a delay in shipment." She also advised Mr. Tcacs not to worry, that his dog would be located and forwarded to his buyer in Cleveland. Mr. Tcacs begged me to intervene and find the bitch, which, although it had sold for five thousand dollars, was uninsured.

My next move was to call the freight supervisor at Red and White. He was unavailable. An hour later he was still unavailable. I telephoned the RCMP and told them I had reason to believe a valuable dog had been stolen from the airport. Twenty minutes later the freight supervisor for the airline called. He was a worried man. The dog had not been misrouted, it had escaped, and had run away from the airport.

Exactly how the white kuvasz had escaped was not clear. The cage may have overturned. It might have been opened by some well-meaning and sympathetic person who thought such a large dog ought to be able to stretch her legs. In any event, once free she had run out of the freight shed, out of the airport, and was last seen crossing Rexdale Boulevard.

Looking at my watch I saw I had exactly ninety minutes of daylight left. I thought I might as well try to find her that same night. I called the Animal Control wardens and the police. My daughter went with me to help as an extra pair of eyes. We drove around until dark, anxiously peering at any white dog that crossed our path, but without success.

At five the next morning I had three vans with drivers, the local shelter manager and myself, all looking for the missing dog. We did find a sheep. Apparently, it had jumped or fallen from a truckload bound for the stockyards. One of our drivers removed it to our farm. We continued our street-by-street check of Rexdale and environs.

By eleven we had found nothing further. We were holding a conference in the middle of the street when an elderly lady came up to us.

"You Humane fellows want to look at the pet store down on that shopping plaza. There's a parrot there that's a disgrace. Its feathers are falling out and it's too weak to move. Something should be done about it."

"Certainly, madam," I replied. "May I have your name and address?"

"What d'you want that for? Won't help the parrot. Why don't you get going." She stomped off.

"Might as well look at the bird, since we are here," I said.

The manager of the shelter, the senior warden and I went to the mall. Finding the pet store, we walked in and stood around the parrot on his perch. He certainly wasn't moving much. He couldn't. He was stuffed. We slunk out.

Feeling I wasn't getting very far, I called a local radio station. The news editor was very helpful and promptly broadcast our story. Within an hour five calls came in from people who had sighted the dog. After checking out each one, two proved to have been about a big white dog on some waste ground off Martin Grove Road. It was Emmy, right enough, but she was so upset she wasn't answering to her name when strangers called her. We could only follow her on foot and in vehicle, trying to keep her in sight.

By two in the afternoon the story had been broadcast three times. Two ladies arrived at the Society's office with a male kuvasz. They were, it proved, from the Kuvasz Club of Canada and keen to help. We drove them and their dog out to Martin Grove Road and chained the handsome male in the back of one of our "catcher" vans, leaving both back doors open.

We backed the van slowly towards the bitch. She was now more excited than upset, true enough, but she hesitated. She wouldn't come any closer than twenty feet.

"Perhaps we're too close," said the manager. "Maybe we humans should back off a bit."

"How could we close the van then?" asked the warden.

I had a brief think. Then I went to a sporting goods shop and bought a roll of fishing line. "Are you after big pike?" the salesman wanted to know. "No, I'm after a big dog," I answered. He gave me a very funny look and a rather careful smile.

We fastened two fifty-yard lengths of fishing line to the back doors of the van, which were hung vertically and closed in the middle. At a cross angle each man, by pulling on his line, could close the door diagonal to him. We sat in cars with the lines through the windows and waited.

Emmy approached, barking and jumping up and down in greeting. As we watched, an Irish setter bitch appeared from nowhere and jumped into the back of the van. After ten seconds of sniffing and tail-wagging, the bitch stood and the kuvasz bred her. We closed the doors. After a while we removed the Irish setter. The kuvasz owners were scandalized.

Once more we propped the van doors open and waited. The male seemed somewhat tired. He was paying less attention to the kuvasz bitch than before. After ten minutes he lay on his blanket with his head on his paws, apparently bored with the whole show. This display of indifference was too much for the female. She ran up to the van and jumped in, licking the male around his head and neck. He made an amazing recovery and was about to stage an encore of his previous performance when we closed the doors. We had secured Emmy.

After we had thanked the Kuvasz Club ladies, I telephoned Red and White Airlines. They were mildly interested. "Bring the dog back, we'll ship it on" was their response.

"Are you prepared to pay the expense the Society had incurred catching this dog?" I asked.

"Well, you see, I've no authority to accept responsibility for anything like that" was the reply I received.

I called the breeder in Calgary. He was delighted. He was not just delighted, he was jubilant. He readily agreed to pay all of our costs. He had only one stipulation: Don't on any account hand Emmy over to Red and White Airlines. Board her at a kuvasz kennel.

He arrived two days later, collected Emmy and set out to deliver her to Cleveland—by car. For once we had a happy ending.

Six months later an ad in the Pet section of a Toronto newspaper caught my eye. It read, "Very large white Irish setter pups for sale. Be among the first in Canada to own one of this little-known breed." The Irish are great salesmen.

THE
GORILLA
IN THE
GARAGE

JIM BRODIE WAS THE CANINE CONTROL OFFICER FOR the townships of Harbord, Pinchum and Horn. Every day, dressed in his World War I officer's uniform, complete with the cracked-leather Sam Brown belt, he would make a tour of the district, mostly chasing dogs that had strayed out of their own backyards. He had a couple of younger men to assist him. Since Jim was fifty-six he preferred to spend most of his time near his kennels, receiving councillors intent on inspecting the premises and intimidating reluctant dog owners into paying the fifteen-dollar fee before they removed their strays.

I knew Jim slightly and had conversed on the telephone with him. I'm not sure if "converse" is the word, since our talks were more like shouting matches. Evidently Jim believed he had to shout to make his voice carry from Landmark to Thornhill.

One day he called me and announced, "It's Brodie. I have to see you. There's a strange beast in Porvale." We agreed to meet the next day at a small eatery on the Porvale main street.

I sat waiting for him at the window table and watched as his yellow-and-black official van mounted the curb before it settled into a parking space.

I ordered coffee for both of us and between sips Jim proceeded to tell of the strange beast. "Last week, one of me lads went after a tan collie in Porvale. It ran into a big garden. Well, they had a big garage. He finally cornered the collie underneath a window at the back of the garage. The window had bars, inside and out. He couldn't help himself but to look in. And what do you think, there were two big eyes looking right back out at him."

"Well, Jim, I can see you'd be curious, but I doubt it's a dog."

"No, but my contract says *all* animals, and it's an animal all right. Anyway, the lad was scared right out of his socks and let the damn dog go."

I asked if he had approached the owners of the strange beast. He shook his head. "Tried to, right enough, but she told me to keep away. None of me business."

"Who is she?"

"Mrs. Leeta Arrowsmith, she calls herself. A right bitch, I reckon. Anyway, the animal's sick. When I went to see her she came out with a needle—penicillin, I guess—and other stuff for it."

I made some notes. Perhaps it was a pet bear that had grown old and dangerous. I decided to phone some of the local vets for information. Likely one of them had treated the animal or prescribed medication for it at some time. The first two I reached were scandalized that I would dare enquire after their patients. The third vet fairly exploded with information.

"Leeta Arrowsmith, I'll say I know her. And her pet bloody gorilla and all." He went on to tell me that she had called him in a year ago when "Gabriel," her nine-year-old gorilla had gone off his feed. Dr. Stollard had had some experience with exotic animals, but Gabriel's problem had eluded him. Not only had Mrs. Arrowsmith declined to pay her bill, but she had abused his wife in a phone call about it. Mrs. Arrowsmith had then arrived in a rage when the surgery was full of small animal patients and their owners, and after some invective that would have caused a bargeman to stand open-mouthed, she had hurled a large stone at the glass door-panel of his office, smashing it completely. He concluded, "She's raving mad, of course."

I swallowed hard. I had a sick gorilla and its nutty owner on my hands. Searching our files I discovered that no one, in the entire history of the Humane Society Movement, had ever seized a gorilla. Not in Massachusetts, not in British Columbia, not even in California. Nowhere. I was to have the dubious distinction of another first.

I discussed the situation with the director.

"It's quite simple," he announced when I outlined the situation. "That gorilla's got to come out of that garage and you've got to make it happen."

"I know," I replied. "The problem is, where do I put it when I've got it out? We can't house it in a retirement home for cats. It certainly won't fit into any of our shelters. The zoo won't have it as a gift, and at the stables it would demolish any loose box. Besides, it would panic the horses for sure."

Looking up the records in the local taxation department, I discovered the owners were a Dr. Sidney Solstice and Mrs. Leeta Arrowsmith, jointly. Dr. Solstice was shown in the medical directory as an obstetrician.

The following day I drove with some trepidation up the drive to the gorilla property. No one was about. The only living things in sight were a pair of squirrels scampering on the lawn. As there was no bell, I knocked on the screen door as loud as the pain in my knuckles would permit. After some moments the door was opened by a tall, thin man with white wavy hair. He had a round face and his expression was benign. His only item of clothing was a bath towel draped round him like a Roman toga.

"Good morning, my clinic's on Wilson, I don't see people here," he announced by way of introduction.

"Dr. Solstice?" I queried.

"Yes," he said. "I've just told you, I don't see people here."

"Well, excuse me," I said, "but I'm not a patient. I've

come to see about the gorilla." I showed him my identification.

"Oh, Gabriel, well in that case come in." He showed me into the living room. He picked up a phone from the top of the television set and dialed a number. "Hello," he said, "there's a man from the Humane Society here about Gabriel. You had better come and talk to him." He turned and smiled at me. "She will be here in a few minutes. I'll get dressed. You can greet her when you see her." I assumed that "she" was Mrs. Arrowsmith.

A few moments later a white van stopped outside the door and a tall woman stepped out, accompanied by two borzoi dogs. The woman had black hair, pulled tightly back and shiny as a raven's wing. Her features were striking. She was almost North American Indian in appearance. She was wearing a tight yellow cashmere sweater and maroon velvet pants, which were tucked into cowboy boots that made her actual five foot nine appear over six feet.

"Hello," she volunteered, "I'm Leeta Arrowsmith."

One of the borzois cocked its leg, wishing to substitute my leg for a tree. I moved away, turning as I did so, thereby losing my balance and striking the dog with my leg.

"You've kicked my dog," snapped Mrs. Arrowsmith.

"Well, he had his leg up to kick me first," I said in a feeble attempt at humour. It fell flat.

"Come this way, please," she said coldly.

We walked to a small door in the garage wall, behind which the loud barking of a big dog was originating.

"I'll just get Dobie out," she said, opening the door. She returned with a very large, very ill-tempered Doberman pinscher, which she quickly chained to a tree. I gave it a wide berth as I moved forward to the garage door.

I stepped inside the building and looked around. My eyes became accustomed to the gloom just in time for me to catch a glimpse of a large, furry ape scuttling out of a barred sleeping cage and into the main part of the garage, which served as an exercise pen. Peering into it through an observation slit, I found myself being observed in return by a large, black, male mountain gorilla. The building smelled of ripe fruit and something else I couldn't identify but didn't like.

The gorilla turned and moved forward on its knuckles. As it did so, I noticed a large greenish-hued sore on its right buttock. Both wet and dried fecal matter adhered to the anal area. The animal's coat was dull, and there were bare, raw patches on its wrists and ankles. Plainly, the wretched creature had eczema over twenty-five percent of its body.

"Have you had a vet to him lately?" I asked.

"Not for some time," she replied. "They won't come for me anymore."

We stepped around a decorated Christmas tree and a small television set arranged so that Gabriel could watch it through his bars. He had been watching *Rollerderby*. There was also, I noted, a neatly made-up single bed and a small fridge in the corner.

"I spend a lot of time with him," Mrs. Arrowsmith went on. "He's my special friend. We want to use him to breed females by artificial insemination."

How the hell does she manage it? I found myself thinking.

Mrs. Arrowsmith must have read my thoughts. "I've handled him daily since he was four. Trouble is, he knows when I'm in the mood before I do and tries to bounce me off the wall. That's how they make love, you know. Trouble is, I'm not a lady gorilla."

We watched Gabriel for some twenty minutes. It was plain to me that the animal wouldn't improve in that garage. He'd have to be removed to more hygienic quarters.

"He'll have to come out of here, Mrs. Arrowsmith," I said at last.

"Nonsense, I can look after him perfectly well right here. All I need is for you to find me a vet. Now you've interfered already, you might as well help me."

We turned to leave. Gabriel scuttled back into his barred sleeping cage, "Uh-uh-uhing" with disgust. The passage between the sleeping cage and the garage outer wall was about two feet wide. Gabriel stuck one of his four-foot-long arms through the bars into the passageway and dared us to try leaving.

I looked back at Mrs. Arrowsmith. She was reciting, sing-song, "Roundy, round the corner, like a teddy bear; one step, two step, and tickly under *there!*" As she spoke she moved a forefinger up the hairy arm to arrive at the beast's armpit on the word "there." The gorilla took his arm into the cage, "eeing," showing his canine teeth and a large expanse of pink gum.

"Thank God, he's ticklish," she said as we arrived at the door.

Outside, the two borzois bounded up to us. "I'll try and get a vet, Mrs. Arrowsmith, but I'm not sure where we can hospitalize him."

She stopped and turned. "He'll only be moved if I approve, you know."

I realized there was no point in trying to reason with her. I would have to make arrangements, then present her with a *fait accompli.* I took my leave. The two borzois urinated on my car wheels as I was trying to manoeuvre round the narrow parking space.

It took ten days and many telephone calls to find a veterinarian willing to take the chance of doctoring a sick gorilla. It took even longer to find a private zoo willing and able to accommodate Gabriel and with facilities to provide the heated cage necessary for him.

Finally, a young professor at a nearby university owned up to having cared for four varieties of apes during his research fellowship. By appointment, we went together to see the gorilla. Mrs. Arrowsmith inspected my doctor friend closely while she smoked a cigarette in a holder. It was long enough to have served a Jivaro Indian as a blowpipe.

"Have you ever treated a gorilla?" Mrs. Arrowsmith asked.

"No," my new friend replied truthfully, "but I *have* treated baboons and chimpanzees. I hope I'll manage all right."

"Perhaps you'd best go down to skid row and dope a few drunks for practice," she suggested.

The young man gave her a forced smile and merely nodded his head.

"I'd like to see where he's going," she went on. "I must approve his quarters before he goes anywhere at all."

At some inconvenience I made arrangements for her to visit the private zoo on a Wednesday. She agreed to phone me late that night after she'd seen it. She didn't phone.

Thursday morning I was up early. Not only did I want to get Gabriel safely out of the garage. I was also in mind of my holiday plans for the following Saturday. Late on Thursday afternoon I was phoning like a bookie's clerk coming down with lockjaw. I assembled a truck, a travelling cage, six men and assorted tools. I also visited a justice of the peace.

Eight o'clock on Friday morning found seven of us and the young vet together at the land adjoining the Arrowsmith property. Shortly, we were joined by a police sergeant and two constables. We moved onto the property and parked in a neat row on the lawn. The vet had brought his entire set of instruments and an oxygen cylinder kit with him, and I had my six strong men. Altogether there were eleven of us and six vehicles.

I walked up to the house and pounded on the door as before. No reply was forthcoming. Accordingly, I elected to carry on with my plans.

I tried the door to the garage and found it locked. Reaching for my wrecking bar, I jimmied the lock and it snapped. Dobie lunged forward, as I knew he would. Stephan, my "dog man," was ready with a catch pole and flicked the soft plastic-covered wire noose over Dobie's snarling head. His teeth were worn and discoloured, but they were still highly dangerous. Stephan tightened the noose and pulled, intending to pull Dobie out of his door much as a wine waiter draws a cork. The dog stubbornly refused to leave.

After more pulling and a fine display of foul language, we discovered the dog was chained to the wall. Someone would have to reach behind him and undo the clip on his collar, thus inviting instant amputation of a finger or two. Since none of my valuable assistants volunteered, I was left to do the job. I allowed Dobie to chomp on a rubber overshoe providentially left in my wagon after the last April storm. After I hastily undid the clip, Stephan succeeded in dragging the outraged dog outside. Dobie was still intent on reducing my overshoe to shreds. As we took stock of the situation, Mrs. Arrowsmith drove up with her borzois.

"What's the meaning of this bloody circus?" she shouted.

"As you can see, we are taking Gabriel away for treatment," I replied civilly.

"Oh no, you don't. You need a court order for that!"

"Well, I just happen to have one here," I countered, taking a folded photocopy of a search warrant out of my shirt pocket.

"Let me see that," she demanded, at the same time snatching the copy. She screwed up her eyes to read, then she tore the paper to shreds, threw them at me and shouted, "Now what are you going to do? There isn't an order anymore!"

"Well, Mrs. Arrowsmith, it happens there is. That was a photocopy you tore up, the real one's in my other pocket." I thanked myself for taking the precaution of carrying a copy.

Mrs. Arrowsmith screamed with rage, "Damn you, damn you!"

I noticed a group of pale-faced neighbours across the road watching from the porch. A mailman also stood there open-mouthed. At this point Dr. Solstice joined the party.

"Now, Leeta, dear," he began.

"Don't you 'Leeta, dear' me! This is your doing, Solly, like when you wrote me those rotten, dirty letters, you bastard." She smacked him on the side of his head, then stood defiantly in the doorway recently vacated by Dobie. "Just try getting in here," she threatened.

"Now, Mrs. Arrowsmith," I said, "you know it's for the best."

She hissed and attempted to knee me between the legs. I dodged, countered by kicking her right shin and turned her around with one arm. The two policemen woke up to the fact that right here before their very eyes was a breach of the peace.

They took an arm each and pushed Mrs. Arrowsmith towards the cruiser. The sergeant opened the back door and Mrs. Arrowsmith was heaved inside. She sat glowering at us through the window.

I gave her a few minutes to cool off before I walked over to the cruiser. "Mrs. Arrowsmith, please won't you help us get Gabriel out?"

"I wouldn't help you. He's better off here." She was still defiant. I left the car.

My biggest inspector had arrived with a jackhammer, as instructed.

"All right, Colin, knock down the end wall," I shouted. The garage wall collapsed in rubble a few moments later.

We inspected the inner door, which was braced with four-by-four timbers. "Better get this lot out of the way," I said, motioning to the bed, fridge, television set and Christmas tree. They were soon arranged on the lawn in as neat a line as the vehicles.

There remained the problem of removing Gabriel to the travelling crate. We solemnly considered shooting him with a tranquillizer dart filled with Serolin. My vet friend was less than enthusiastic.

"It might do more harm than good," he said. "I'd much rather do it by hand."

Eventually, we elected to try driving the gorilla into his sleeping cage, where he could be reached through the bars with a hypodermic needle. We tempted him with a bunch of bananas I'd brought with me. No response. I sent one of the troops to a fruit shop for a basket of peaches. Gabriel ignored them completely.

We thought about it while we each sucked a juicy peach. Mrs. Arrowsmith wouldn't have one. The policemen, "thank you very much," would.

Finally, Phillip, my zoo friend, whose first love is big cats, and not gorillas, made one of his rare speeches. "They're afraid of water in the wild. Let's splash some water at him, it's better than nothing."

We filled several paper cups and carefully pulled away the timber from the pen door. Phillip and I stood ready, each with cups of water in our hands. The bolts were slipped and the door opened. Phillip and I aimed and threw together.

Gabriel scurried into his sleeping cage, "uh-uhing" angrily. We beamed congratulations at each other. My veterinarian friend broke the spell.

"If you can just back him against the bars, I can get the needle into him."

Gabriel squatted in the centre of his cage, regarding us solemnly with his deep-set black eyes, looking for all the world like a hairy Buddha. I picked up a broom. Perhaps I could chase him down the cage with it. Gabriel looked at the broom apathetically. He didn't move. I prodded him with it. He yawned. I pushed harder. He regarded me with little more than a passing interest. I swung the broom in an arc, swatting him. He languidly stuck out one arm and seized the broom, holding it impassively. I tried to pull the broom from him. I couldn't budge it. I sweated and heaved again, with the same result. Colin, the largest inspector, joined me at the broom handle. Gabriel appeared to be contemplating the fingernails of one hand while idly holding onto the broom with the other. Stephan, two hundred pounds of Ukrainian working weight, joined us. The broom handle might just as well have been Excalibur stuck in the stone.

We were still pulling when Gabriel evidently tired of playing with us. Slowly he pulled the broom handle into his cage. We had a choice: we could let go or be dragged between the bars. We let go.

More water was called for. Our vet positioned himself beside the pen. We splashed more water. The ape backed into a corner. The needle went home. We relaxed. The vet, strangely, did not.

"Now what's the problem?" I asked.

"I'm just not sure of the dosage," he said, not taking his eyes off Gabriel. "I may have given him too much, in which case he's had it, or not enough, in which case he may wake up while we're moving him."

"Tell me when he's under," I replied. "We haven't any time to waste."

Gabriel sat in the centre of his cage, his eyes becoming glassier and glassier. I decided to sacrifice another broom. I pushed him with it, took a playful whack at him. There was no response.

Phillip and I unbolted the door, walked in, seized Gabriel by his arms, draped one each around our necks and staggered out of the cage like three old drunks.

When we reached the travelling crate, we saw that the open hatch was much too small for Gabriel. He'd have to go in through the large open end. The trouble was that it was padlocked. Melvyn, Phillip's assistant, looked through his keys for a likely one, anxiously trying one key after another. Phillip and I continued promenading Gabriel round and round the lawn.

Mrs. Arrowsmith screamed something at us out of the police car. I wished I were on a beach somewhere eating a peach with my trousers rolled.

At this point, Brodie arrived, uncharacteristically late. I had wondered where he was.

"Ha ha, well done, lads. So you got him out and all. Fine, fine, just stick him in here and I'll trundle him off home."

He opened the back of his battered van to expose a double Greyhound carrying cage. Ill as he was, Gabriel would have used it like Plasticene, not that Brodie's jurisdiction extended to Gabriel's case in the first place. But clearly he thought it did.

I was in no mood for humouring anyone at this stage. "Oh shove off, Jim," I said, casting an anxious eye on Melvyn, who was feverishly trying still more keys in the cage padlock. Phillip was more to the point.

"For Pete's sake, hurry up, Mel," he shouted. "This thing's coming round." He was right. Gabriel was beginning to roll his head, grimace and slaver all over us.

"Now, just a minute," insisted Brodie. "I'm in charge of all animals in this township." He tried to pull Gabriel's right arm off Phillip. "Now let go will you!"

A chorus of protest made him stop. Then he moved again. Big Colin moved. There was a thump. Brodie was flat on his back. Colin had knocked him out. The police realized there was another breach of the peace to deal with. Brodie joined Mrs. Arrowsmith in the rear of the cruiser, weakly protesting his innocence.

At this point, Mel got the lock open. We thrust Gabriel inside, none too soon. He came awake banging his chest.

Dr. Solstice came back, his right ear noticeably red.

"I say, if you want to give him anything, you should put it in a chocolate Turtle. He'll do anything for Turtles. I give them to him all the time."

"Thank you," I said, "but we've managed."

He smirked at Mrs. Arrowsmith. "They got you at last, I see." Mrs. Arrowsmith's baleful gaze promised more assault when she was free.

We heaved the steel travelling crate containing Gabriel onto the truck platform, elevated the platform and secured the crate to the floor. We were ready to leave.

The police sergeant approached me. "What do you want to do with these two?" he asked.

"Oh, release them when we've gone, please," I replied. "I've no wish to charge them."

He seemed just a tiny bit piqued.

We delivered the men and tools to their various stations. The truck with Gabriel in it left for the friendly, private zoo. As we drove along after it, the vet and I talked the case over.

"He's pretty sick, you know," the vet said. "The skin condition is the worst I've ever seen and that wound is gangrenous."

"What do you think would cause that? He obviously picks at it, but it didn't start that way. There's a funny smell in that garage, too," I said. I was still puzzled by that and I still didn't like it.

We arrived at the zoo, where Gabriel was given another dose of Serolin and unloaded. A patient group of animal handlers stood ready in overalls and rubber boots. Gabriel was secured by two ropes around his shoulders, leading back through the crate, the ends held by very large men. This was a safety precaution: if Gabriel should suddenly recover, he could be pulled backwards into the cage. The rest of the gang, with pails of soapy water and car-washing brushes, set about washing him clean. When clean, he was dried with bath towels and put to bed on deep, deep straw in a quiet air-conditioned barn. Our vet and the zoo's resident vet fed him intravenously and gave him plasma as well. He slept like a baby.

The next few days Gabriel was nursed day and night. He did not improve, but steadily declined. I was away on holiday but phoned in every day to check on his condition. A week later I was saddened to hear he was in a coma. On Saturday morning he was dead.

Both vets wanted a post-mortem examination done, so the body was shipped to the teaching university's eminent veterinary department. Our two vets were there that Sunday afternoon, of course. And no less than eight professors of pathology left their golf, their swimming pools, and their barbeques to seek the cause of this magnificent animal's death.

They opened up the body, removed organs and innards till the remains looked like a dugout canoe. Gabriel had had cirrhosis of the liver, pancreatitis, stomach ulcers, an enlarged heart, gangrene in one buttock, and ulcerated wrist and ankles, but no one thing that would have killed him. I asked for a whole range of tests on hair, skin and organs. Specimens were taken.

Two weeks later the results were known. Thalumine poisoning! Common rat poison, consumed in large amounts, had killed Gabriel. How? Gorillas don't readily eat anything but fruit and leaves. Risking life and limb, I went back to call on Mrs. Arrowsmith.

She answered the door subdued and tearful, wearing a heavy black mourning dress. She sobbed and said little as I talked to her. I told her what we had found. She cried some more, finally nodded, and spoke.

"I had a tough time controlling him as he grew older. When I needed to handle him for semen training, I gave him Atravet (a drug) in vodka. It used to put him down for an hour or so while I got in with him. After a while he got like an alcoholic waiting for his drink. I'm not sure about the poison, but I think I know."

I looked at her. "It was Dr. Solstice, wasn't it?" I asked.

"Yes," she replied, "we've been lovers for years, but we've broken up. He was jealous of Gabriel."

I puzzled to myself on the way home. What kind of man would be jealous enough to poison his mistress's pet gorilla?

This small tragedy had begun not in a garage but nine years earlier, when Gabriel's mother was shot in the Congo and he was snatched from her arms. It ended in Canada, the last place God would have placed gorillas. They ought to be left in Africa. Exotic species belong in their native environments. Man's dominion over the beasts of the earth includes a responsibility to preserve them in their own habitat.

THE NATIONAL BESTSELLER
OVER ONE MILLION COPIES IN PRINT

Warm and Wonderful Stories
about the Animals Herriot Loves Best

"HERRIOT'S SKILL AS A
STORYTELLER IS CLASSIC."
—DETROIT FREE PRESS

JAMES HERRIOT'S DOG STORIES
_____ 90143-7 $4.95 U.S.